Season of the Gar

Season of the Gar

Adventures in Pursuit of America's
Most Misunderstood Fish

Mark Spitzer

The University of Arkansas Press
Fayetteville
2010

Copyright © 2010 by The University of Arkansas Press

ISBN-10: 1-55728-929-8
ISBN-13: 978-1-55728-929-2

14   13   12   11   10   5   4   3   2   1

Text design by Ellen Beeler

⊗ The paper used in this publication meets the minimum requirements of
the American National Standard for Permanence of Paper for Printed Library
Materials Z39.48-1984.

Library of Congress Cataloging-in-Publication Data

Spitzer, Mark, 1965–
    Season of the gar : adventures in pursuit of America's most misunderstood
    fish / Mark Spitzer.
         p. cm.
    Includes bibliographical references.
    ISBN 978-1-55728-929-2 (pbk. : alk. paper)
    1. Alligator gar—United States—Gulf States Region. I. Title.
    QL638.L4S65 2010
    597'.66—dc22

                                                                                2009053364

To my wife Robin

and the most fantastic

fish on the planet

Contents

Gar Images

Preface

To stereotype my gar-obsession:

Back when I was a gar-virgin, I could hardly do anything other than research and write about gar, fish for gar, and dream about gar—so as to become gar-experienced. It was a long time coming, but it finally happened, and in the process, I lost my gar-innocence, which allowed my monomania ("Gar Fever") to finally release its hold on me.

The result is a book devoted to a subject in which the imagination has always been a major factor. For millennia, gar have inspired myths, legends, scenes of slaughter, extreme emotions, epic battles, and in the tradition of ye olde fish story, extravagant lies.

Concerning the latter, I would like to make it clear that there is only one moment in the following pages that is not as truthful as it pretends to be. This happens at the end of the first chapter when my hairy Bulgarian accomplice and I take on a monster-gar in the swamps of Louisiana, where there are no Gaspergou Bayou Oil and Gas Fields. The reason that I mention this is because—in these days of James Frey and the dialogue regarding where to sincerely draw the line between fiction and nonfiction—it's important for writers to honor the unofficial contract with their readers not to stray from their expectations. At the time that I wrote that piece, though, this wasn't a concern of mine. But now, since one of the missions of this book is to comment on our tendency to indulge in misinformation, I indicate this in the interest of offering the most honest and credible text that I can on a topic tainted by false information. That said, the rest of this book can be trusted not to twist the facts beyond the generally acceptable degree of tinkering with minor details.

Now that that's cleared up, I would like to note that even though I learned a lot about gar in the metaphorical season I spent on this project (which started out in Louisiana, ran its course through Missouri and Texas, and ended up in Arkansas), there's still a lot I don't know, and there's still a lot the experts don't know. But that's why gar have always been intriguing: They are true mystery fish, whose histories have been confused by sloppy scholarship, unchecked science, prejudicial journalism, and generations of fishermen who think they know the facts.

Another message in this book is that gar aren't as destructive to other fish as they've been made out to be, and that they serve a valuable function in providing ecological balance. Plus, contrary to popular belief, gar do not destroy gamefish populations or eat their own weight (or twice their own weight) in other fish per day. As studies have shown, gar cut down on populations of carp, shad, drum, buffalo, and other fish that can be destructive to nesting habitats, therefore leaving the smaller members of the minnow family for bass, pike, catfish, trout, crappie, et cetera.

Though it sometimes might feel as if the purpose of this book is to glorify a demonized fish, it is not my intention to portray garfish as victims. Rather, this book seeks to "re-educate" (more on this term later) humans on the issues involving gar, in order to help protect and preserve a fascinating natural resource.

This book is not a nature book, nor is it a fishing book, or even a study. If anything, it's a creative nonfiction montage of different voices with varying tones, all grounded in the central theme of *my* relationship with gar—which I use to reflect *our* relationship with gar. Thus, the following pages contain essays, folklore, what I call "garticles," comic relief, flashes of science, unavoidable bias, recipes, a portrait of a pet gar, a first-person narrative thread leading to the fulfillment of a lifelong dream, a look at changing management plans and garfishing/bowhunting laws, and a heavily footnoted regional history included for its timely information on propagating gator gar. In other words, these chapters are multi-faceted, just like gar are.

And since there are white gar, black gar, gray gar, brown gar, gold gar, green gar, yellow gar, fat gar, skinny gar, old gar, young gar, stripy gar, spotty gar, one-eyed gar, gars with chinked scales, gars with bullet holes in their fins, gars with scarred-up lumps on their heads, gars galore, it follows that every individual gar is just as unique as every individual human. And since gar are not out to get us, and since gar are spectacular sport fish to do battle with, and since their meat is good to eat (when they're not full of PCBs, DDT, and other poisonous acronyms), and since gar are a dwindling constant in our ever-threatened environment, as well as fellow mutants just trying to survive on this rapidly changing planet, it's time to change our attitude. Especially concerning the alligator gar, which is officially "imperiled" throughout its range.

Which leads me to an issue in Arkansas, where it looked like the Game & Fish Commission was going to pass a package of laws to protect the state's largest populations of gator gar. Unfortunately, by the time this book went to press, no refuge areas had been approved. Still, a free permit was put into effect (a reduced creel limit of one per day) with a moratorium on harvest for any alligator gar more than three feet long during spawning season (May and June).

Whereas some might view these changes as progress, this failure to completely protect these fish bummed me out for two reasons in particular. First, because these gar are highly endangered, so, therefore, are in need of serious protection; and second, because I may have revealed clues to their waterways in this book which I hoped wouldn't matter, since they'd be protected.

Having agonized for months, however, about whether to fictionalize the names of certain rivers, I ultimately decided that I needed to keep my information as accurate as possible. Besides, it's not like the whereabouts of these fish haven't been published and posted by others in the past; that information is already out there.

Hence, I'm optimistic that the spirit of this book can add more to the general consciousness of what's going on regarding gar than it might take away by directing those who would do gar harm to places where their populations hang in the balance. Needless to say, this is a risky bet, as well as one that makes the situation even more urgent.

No doubt, though, I'm preaching (for the most part) to a choir that already respects the fact that we need to do more to protect America's most misunderstood fish in order to preserve what's left of our world as we know it. Call me idealistic, call me a fool, I don't care. But if you use this book to locate and hunt alligator gar in Arkansas, then before you take that shot . . . remember the regional fishing guides from the '50s that you'll read about in this book. Then recall their regrets, and consider what we've been trying to recover from for over half a century, and weigh that with the certainty that if you subtract that fish from its gene pool, then your powers of denial better be strong enough to convince yourself (and your children) that the momentary thrill you experience will be worth lessening the chances all future generations will ever have of having a choice in the matter of what's more important to sacrifice: the *selfish* urge to kill a fish, or a vanishing part of our ecosystem teetering on the brink of extinction.

Meaning garocide is suicide, so SAVE THE GAR—for ourselves.

—Mark Spitzer, 2009.

Acknowledgments

Work in this book has appeared in *Ecotone, Black Warrior Review, Yale Anglers Journal, Clackamas Literary Review, Big Muddy, The Chariton Review, Rougarou,* and the books *Tight Lines* (Yale University Press, 2007) and *Riding the Unit* (Six Gallery Press, 2006). Thanks to Rustin Gooden, Steve Ryan, James Cianciola, Don Jones, and the American Museum of Natural History for photo permissions. Keith "Catfish" Sutton was extremely helpful with this book, supplying tons of information and some highly suspect fish stories. My gratitude also to Kirk Kirkland, Eric Tumminia (Hippy), Rex Rose, Robin Becker, David Gessner, Nina de Gramont, Tom Lavoie, Lawrence Malley, Katy Henriksen, Pamela Hill, Brian King (and everyone else at the University of Arkansas Press), Leon Bisher, Steve Johnson, Burl Cain, Barry McFarland, Kevin P.Q. Phelan, Plamen Arnaudov, Kris Hansen, Andrei Codrescu, Roger Kamenetz, Christopher Kennedy, Neil H. Shubin, Alysse Ferrara, David Buckmeier, Adam Petry, Chris Turner, Matthew Bokovoy, Kirk Bjornsgaard, Jeff Porter, W.P. Meyer, William Louvou, Doug Stange, Lee Holt, William Layher, Ed Kluender, Tommy Inebnit, Reid Adams, Ted Frushour, Jeremy Wade, Bubba Bedre, Sparky Romine, Tim Thornes, and everyone and everyfish who contributed to this project.

1

Getting a Garfish

"It lies sometimes asleep or motionless on the surface of the water and may be mistaken for a log or snag. It is impossible to take it in any other way than with the seine or a very strong hook; the prongs of the gig cannot pierce the scales, which are as hard as flint . . . They strike fire with steel and are ball-proof!"

—C.S. RAFINESQUE.

"It has a bad reputation, and there is a difference of opinion concerning its value."

—EDWARD C. MIGDALSKI.

I T WAS THOSE PICTURES in fish books I saw as a kid. Particularly that one of two guys in Arkansas, posing beside a ferocious, steely alligator gar longer than themselves. According to Maynard Reece's *Fish and Fishing* (1963), their hook was rigged to a piano string; but according to my imagination, what they used for bait was a whole chicken. So that's why I wanted to get a gar.

Growing up in Minnesota, though, there weren't too many gar around. Living in the Colorado Rockies and France in my twenties also didn't help. But in my early thirties, I went back to graduate school, this time in Louisiana, where people still fish for gar. And bowhunt them. And eat them. That is, if they're not despised for belonging to that ichthyological underclass of scavengers known as "trash fish," the enemies of game fish.

One reason I wanted to get a gar was to get a good look at *le poisson armé* (the armored fish), as the French explorers called it back in the 1700s. I wanted to check out that prehistoric alligator head, those razor-sharp fangs,

1

and that serpentine body dating back to the Paleozoic—making garfish (along with coelacanth, bowfin, and sturgeon) one of the oldest living fish families on the planet.

So I asked a tire-repair guy in Lafayette where I could catch a "Cajun barracuda" (as they're sometimes called in Acadiana), and he told me to find Old Henderson Road and drive out to where it dead ends at a rotting bridge. The gar swam so thick there, he told me, that I could pick out the biggest one and drop some bait in front of it. He also advised taking a jack handle along for calming them down once I got them up on the bridge.

It didn't take long to find the spot. I went out there, looked down, and sure enough, a skinny, snaky gar was swimming on the surface, snapping sideways at bugs because of its peripheral vision. It was the first wild gar I had ever seen, and it was hungry. So I dropped my worm in front of it, steel leader and everything. The gar bit, I fought it, it got away. And though I went back to that spot at least thirty times, and even managed to hook a few, I could never seal the deal.

But I did get familiar with the Atchafalaya Basin, driving around on the levees, going to bars with six-foot gator gars mounted on the walls

White River gar, Arkansas. This fish weighed 230 pounds and was seven feet eight inches long. The photograph appeared on postcards in the late '50s. This picture sparked the author's imagination, leading to a lifelong gar fascination. Photo by Johnnie M. Gray.

(like the two-hundred-pounder at McGee's), and fishing in the cypress swamps—where locals told me to use a piece of frayed nylon rope so their teeth get tangled in the fibers.

For years, I tried all sorts of methods. But I just couldn't get the barbs to stick.

The size of gar has been greatly exaggerated. For some reason, the mythical figure of twenty feet is associated with the alligator gar, the largest of its species. In *The Angler's Guide to the Fresh Water Sport Fishes of America* (1962), for example, Edward C. Migdalski writes, "Many huge sizes have been recorded by word of mouth; even statements of '20 feet long' . . . have been published in past years by reputable scientists." Similarly, *Fishes and Fishing in Louisiana*, published by the Louisiana Department of Conservation in 1933, notes that the "Mississippi Alligator Gar" attains "a length of as much as twenty feet." J. R. Norman, in *A History of Fishes* (1948), then repeats this misinformation, noting that "the Alligator Gar Pike" can reach "a length of twenty feet or more."

Fossil records indicate that millenniums ago garfish got close to fifteen feet. According to Migdalski, such behemoths existed on this continent during the last few centuries: "Twelve and 14-foot monsters . . . lived many years ago in areas such as lower Arkansas, Mississippi, and Louisiana where little or no fishing took place. Undoubtedly, many huge gars were captured and not recorded or shot and allowed to sink . . . it didn't take long before the real big fellows disappeared from the scene."

These days, however, the truth is that gator gar are physically capable of reaching lengths of ten feet if allowed to grow for more than forty years. But reports of such gar are unverified and mostly come from legends —like the 1818 description by Constantine Rafinesque, which claims their "length is from 4 to 10 feet." This figure agrees with the brunt of scientific data, as in "Species Summary for Atractosteus spatula," published on a biology-based museum website, which states that the maximum size for gar is "304.8 cm." Still, modern gar hardly ever exceed seven feet, though eight-foot gator gar have been reported in Louisiana, Texas, Mississippi, Missouri, Arkansas, and Oklahoma during the last century.

Nevertheless, there's a dispute about the length of the world-record garfish. According to Migdalski's figures from the 1960s, it was a nine-foot-nine gar; but according to the Earthwave Society's 2001 Garsite, it was seven and a half feet long. This same lunker gar is referred to in

"Division of Fisheries Facts about Fish in the Southwest" (an article posted on a website of the U.S. Fish and Wildlife Service), where it's reported that the "largest known individual was 10 feet long."

The only consistent thing we know about this gar is its weight. According to most sources, it was 302 pounds.

But there have been reports of heavier gar. According to John James Audubon, a gar "was caught which weighed 400 pounds." Other sources echo this figure, but the facts remain a bit fishy, with hearsay and rumor carrying more weight than official statistics.

The best evidence of garfish monstrosity is photographs. Like the one in *Killers of the Seas* (1973) by Edward R. Ricciuti, showing a bunch of Depression-era men in overalls and hats, smoking cigs on a cobblestoned

Little Rock, circa 1928. Photo courtesy of the American Museum of Natural History.

Little Rock street. Beneath the glow of an old-time street lamp, a lunker gar is strapped to the bumper of a rickety truck. This fish appears to be about seven feet long.

Or in the magazine *In-Fisherman,* in an article titled "Gar Wars," there's a popular photo from the '30s of a safari-hatted Dr. Drennen cranking back on his rod while L. E. Piper pulls back on a bow, arrow poised and ready for release, pointing straight toward the head of a surface-bursting gator gar. The head of this fish is twice the size of the doctor's.

I also have a photo of Barbara Roy and her "unofficial state record garfish" (supposedly caught on twenty-pound test) hanging beside her. She "caught [this] monster Garfish on her new Zebco 888 rod & reel," according to Cajun Charlie, who sent the picture to *Louisiana Fishing Magazine.* This gar is two heads higher than Barbara Roy, and she's no midget.

My favorite picture, however, will always be the one of that White River gar in Arkansas, which weighs well over two hundred pounds and is as fat around as a trash can. It lies on the sand while the fishermen raise

Mississippi Alligator Gar. This supposed ten-footer is reported to have been caught in Moon Lake, Mississippi, in 1910. Some experts challenge the legitimacy of this photograph because the stomach seems to be more slack than usual (for its size) and the fins and tail are unnaturally flared. Photo by D. Franklin. Courtesy of the American Museum of Natural History, image # 117075.

its head, showing off its nostrils and fangs. This is the famous photo that first made me ask, "What the hell kind of fish is that?"

On a bayou by Breaux Bridge, a four-foot gar was hooked on a line someone had strung from an overhanging branch. It was flopping around, just twenty yards away by the opposite bank. I could've swum across and risked being caught by whoever set that line (an unforgivable offense in Cajun country), but since I didn't feel like braving the water-moccasined current, I just sat there and watched it splash.

Another time, I was out on Alligator Bayou east of Baton Rouge, drinking beer with my buddy Kris Hansen. The water was low, and the gar were rolling in the weeds as they do throughout the summer. Kris had a ridiculous oversized lure. It was red and white and looked like a beer can, and every time he cast it out a longnose hit it. He couldn't set the hook, though, because their beaks were too bony for the barbs to catch.

After that, below Plaquemine, one followed my girlfriend's bobber in. We could see it on the surface, its long, skinny body tinted gold by the copper water. If I would've had a gun at the time, I would've had a garfish.

Over by Lake Fardoche, I saw one leap completely out of the water, twist in the sky, then slap down on its side. That gar was longer than most men.

But on the levee below Henderson, on rutted roads heading through the brush, that's where I'd find giant piles of dead gar, their bellies slit open, meat scraped out, heads cooked clean by the sun. These were the spoils of gar fishermen who dumped gar-heaps by the truckload, sometimes leaving cadaver-piles three to five feet tall.

On one of these roads, I discovered a bunch of gar heads. The first was the hugest I had ever seen, taken off a fish measuring at least six feet. The second one was even bigger. But the third one was the biggest of them all! At first I thought it was an alligator skull.

I took it home and threw it on the roof so the sun could dry it out. Meanwhile, I compared the size of this head to the one at Prejean's, a restaurant north of Lafayette. Their trophy gar was six-foot-something and two hundred-plus pounds. My gar skull was almost twice the size of theirs, making it a gar of unspeakable proportions.

I eventually wrapped that gar head up, drove it out to New Mexico, and gave it to my father. He thought it was pretty cool, too, so he put it on a stump outside the kitchen window. It didn't take long for the coyotes to find it and run off into the foothills. Now, somewhere in the arroyos of the Sangre de Cristos (the land of delicate trout), there's an incredible fish head bleached by the sun, its wolfy canines grinning at the sky.

Getting a garfish has not been easy. I've been down in the swamps for years now and have pretty much given in to the conviction that it takes someone raised on dirty rice and jambalaya to hook a gar. There are flaws to this argument, of course, since people from all over come to these parts and catch garfish by accident—like Japanese tourists going for redfish in the Gulf (because gar can live in salt water too, e.g., the two six-footers swimming with the sharks at the New Orleans Aquarium).

My point is this: Midwestern fishermen can't catch gar, since it's a different kind of fishing than sitting on the shore and staring at a bobber. Garfishing involves trotlines, special nets and, in the case of alligator gar, heavy-duty equipment. But it also involves a tolerance to the heat which Sven and Ollie will never develop, but which Boudreaux and Thibodeaux have become accustomed to. Since southerners have developed a genetic disposition to the heat of the day in the summer (when gar are most active), they can get out there and get them. But when northerners go out on an August afternoon and it's 110 degrees, they get dizzy from the blazing rays, and after a couple of hours they dehydrate into jerky.

Admittedly, this theory is not grounded in scientific research; it's founded on fishing frustration, the vast general statement, and the convenience of making stereotypes.

The fish books agree on our lack of information regarding gar, noting that for the amount of time this fish has been around, we should know way more than we do—especially considering their vast demographics. Garfish once covered an area from Canada down to South America, and only a century ago they covered half the continent. This raises the question of why they weren't observed more, and studied more, in the 1800s.

The answer, however, is obvious: Gar are valued less than the common lab rat. To most eyes that do not wonder at the amazing ganoid structure of their diamond-shaped armor, their fossilific jaws and needle-sharp incisors, garfish are not beautiful creatures. I once served some gar steaks to the writer Andrei Codrescu, but he refused to eat them, claiming, "That fish is just too ugly, man." This reinforced what I saw as the popular attitude toward garfish, which explains its stigma. Basically, hardly anyone loves a garfish. Therefore, hardly anyone cares about gar—which has affected our knowledge of the species.

As Bob Pitman of the U.S. Fish and Wildlife Service notes in Craig Springer's article "Gearing Up for Alligator Gar," "It's just ironic. . . . Here we have the second largest freshwater fish in the US, and yet we know so little about it." Springer then adds, "The body of knowledge on alligator gar is indeed very limited. Life history studies are lacking. To date, studies on alligator gar have been confined to diet, with some cursory inquiries on the fish's distribution in a few of the states."

Similarly, Migdalski's *Angler's Guide* argues that our lack of gar knowledge is reflected by an ambiguous taxonomy: "Authors of technical works on freshwater fishes state, 'there are fewer than ten species' or 'the gar family contains about ten species.' This indecisiveness about a basic fact indicates how little we know about this family."

Within the last three decades, though, biologists and conservationists, along with government agencies, have been making efforts to study gar. The majority of these authorities are united in their befuddlement over the great decline in gar populations, frequently citing "overfishing" as the most likely reason for their plummeting numbers, while bemoaning the fact that there is no hard evidence for this hypothesis. Since gar are becoming more and more of a rarity (and therefore a novelty), sportfishing has also been suggested as a cause for their dwindling populations. Still, there has not yet been a consensus that garfishing contributes to extinction.

A more compelling argument is that of mass extermination, which was encouraged by anti-garfish propaganda from the '30s. For example, government publications like *Fishes and Fishing in Louisiana* didn't help the gar's reputation by printing statements such as: "The Gars, so familiar an element in our Louisiana fish fauna, are of unusual interest for many reasons. Numbered among our most objectionable fishes, they are a pest to the commercial fisherman and to the angler alike, for their voracity are responsible for the destruction of great numbers of useful and valuable fishes."

Or, as *In-Fisherman* points out, "Historical records verify a persistent campaign to eradicate alligator gar. As early as 1933, writers called for their destruction . . . [claiming] they are a menace to modern animal life and will wreak vast destruction unless they themselves are destroyed by game lovers and sportsmen alike." *A History of Fishes* repeats this sentiment, noting that "The Alligator Gar Pike . . . is very destructive to food fishes, and causes a great deal of damage to the nets of fishermen, who kill it without mercy. It is not even good eating itself, the flesh being rank and tough, and unfit even for dogs."

This overall attitude toward garfish, along with other unstudied accusations and rumors of plague (like various "parasitic mussel" scares, in which gar were falsely villainized as carriers), eventually led to their classification as "garbage fish" in close to half the states in America by the middle of the twentieth century. In fact, up until the 1990s, most states had no set limit on the taking of gar. Some states even made it illegal to return gar to the water and called upon fishermen to destroy them. The result is severely diminished populations in the North, and basically, gar have disappeared from the West, where water is less plentiful now.

A quarter-century of research, however, has revealed that garfish pose little threat to gamefish populations (i.e., bass, pike, walleye, trout, catfish, etc.). It used to be believed that gar destroy the nesting grounds of other species to propagate their own, but this misinformation has been refuted by recent studies that explain how gar spawn in warm, shallow backwaters, which higher-status fish usually avoid.

Also, as *Food Study of the Bowfin and Gars in Eastern Texas* (published by the Texas Parks and Wildlife Department, 1971) established, the diet of garfish consists mainly of forage fish—which are defined as shiners, shad, suckers, chubs, carp, gou (sheepshead), bullheads, buffalo, bowfin, gar (yep, they eat their own kind), and other types of "rough fish" generally considered abundant and disposable. This study was conducted at various points from 1963 to 1966 and relied on data extracted from the bellies of bowfin and gar, which share similar diets. Here are some findings collected from February 1, 1964, to January 31, 1965: "Out of 240 specimens collected, 165 had food in their stomachs. No bugs were discovered, but 23 crustaceans (mostly crawfish) were, along with 302 forage fish. There were 63 unidentified remains, 0 amphibians, 3 instances of detritus (vegetation, sticks, small grains and artificial lures), 4 instances of 'unidentified' (meaning completely unknown food items, due to high degrees of digestion), and 13 gamefish." This means that only 5 percent of all gar examined in this study had ingested game fish. No doubt, most of these were sunfish, which are even more common in the diet of game fish.

Such figures were found to be consistent with other studies conducted in the '70s and '80s, making it official that the amount of game fish devoured by gar is minimal. Hence, the argument that gar are destroyers of game fish has been proven false, and it has also been established that garfish play a vital role in controlling carp and other large minnows, which are much more harmful to gamefish populations than gar are.

As states like Arkansas looked at their endangered species lists in light of this new information, they began to pass laws to protect alligator gar. Throughout the '90s, most southern states incorporated new limits (sometimes as low as two per day), while repealing laws mandating their destruction. Oklahoma started tagging them in order to track them and understand their habits, and using hatcheries to bring their numbers up. The Tennessee Wildlife Resources Agency enacted legislation against gator gar harvesting, in the interest of developing "constructive management plans that do not regard alligator gar as nuisances to be destroyed, but as beneficial predators that contribute positively to ecosystem stability, the balance among predators and prey, and . . . exciting angling."

Nevertheless, the experts agree that something beyond overfishing, sportfishing, and encouraging eradication has been a factor in vanishing garfish populations—but they don't know what it is. When they come to me, though, I'll give them this three-part answer:

> **1) Continental Constipation:** Like salmon, like squawfish, like half the freshwater fish on the planet, garfish can't swim as far upstream as they used to, because of dams. And since dams control flooding, and since there is now less flooding than there used to be, and since garfish migrate, there are now fewer places for gar to spawn. Plus, dams affect water temperature, and all it takes is a difference of a few degrees to make gar less willing to spawn.
>
> **2) Delicate Reproduction:** Since garfish spawning is now pretty much relegated to the marshy backwaters and swamps of the South (thanks to the above), flood plains are required where water levels do not fluctuate, so that gar eggs can remain under water for three to nine days to hatch. The jettisoning of eggs is a sensitive process, depending on specific plant life for the fry to attach to after they are born. The newborn fish then need about a week to live off their egg sacs before they can leave the spawning grounds. Increased farming and development have been hampering this process.
>
> **3) Insecticides, Fertilizers, and Other Poisons:** As numerous studies have proven, DDT and other chemicals get into animal fat, where traces remain for generations, softening the outer layers of eggs, causing sterility and the degeneration of immune s   y   s   t   e   m   s in various species—particularly those at the top of the food chain, because of their consumption of compromised prey. There has

been a nationwide ban on DDT for decades now, thanks to conservationist consternation concerning contamination, and infected animal populations have been making a comeback across the country. Tests on gar roe would no doubt find insecticides and other pollutants, but the lowly garfish is never tested.

So after all that book learning, it was time to finally get a garfish. My bruised fishing ego was at stake. That's why I was taking my friend Kevin to the levee again.

The day before, we had been out there catching minnows to feed to my pet bullhead when we stumbled across a gar-spawning spot. The water was high, and they were rolling in the grass in the afternoon heat. I had to get one!

Wading out with my minnow net, I began stalking gar. They let me get pretty close, and I could see them clearly; they were a couple feet long with oblong black spots, swimming in groups of two to five. Must've been fifty or sixty of them.

I'd get as close as I could, but then they'd shoot off. I'd plunge in my net and miss every time. Until I snuck up on a stump, where I could see a couple on the other side, rolling in the weeds. The smart one saw me and shot away, but the dumb one stayed behind. That garfish was a sitting duck.

I positioned the net right over its head, and went for it. SPLASHHH! The garfish shot straight into it. I pulled the net up on the stump, and the gar came with it, splashing like crazy. I had it. It was mine. Finally, a garfish!

But then it flopped out of the net and started slapping around on the stump. I dove for it, slipped, and fell into the muck, allowing the garfish to slap back into the bayou.

That's why we were heading back. This time, though, I was armed with a brand new net, which I had reinforced and extended with a mop handle.

"*Lepisosteus*," I told Kevin as I drove, "is known by many names: gar pike, gator gar, diamond-fish, devil-fish, jackfish, garjack, bony pike, billy gar, et cetera."

Kevin didn't seem to be very impressed. He lit up a cig while I continued:

"Garfish have lunglike organs that breathe air. This allows them to lie in muddy creek beds and wait for the rains, or gulp air on the surface of low-oxygen ponds."

I was an encyclopedia of fascinating gar facts:

"The roe of garfish is toxic to humans and animals. Some Native American tribes once made arrowheads from their scales. There's a saying in the Carolinas which goes 'as common as gar-broth.'"

"What do they eat?" Kevin asked, blowing out a plume of smoke.

"Mostly big minnows," I told him, "but also ducks, bugs, herons, crawfish, and nutria rats. Some have allegedly eaten soap, as well as turkeys, small dogs, boat parts, and decoys."

"What about humans?"

"There's never been a verified account," I answered, totally prepared for this question, "but there have been reports of maulings. The most famous is from 1932, in Mandeville, Louisiana, at the height of American garanoia. A certain Dr. Paine reported that he had patched up a nine-year-old girl who'd been sitting on the edge of Lake Pontchartrain, dangling her feet in the water. Her toes must've looked like teeny weenies, because the next thing she knew a seven-foot gar was dragging her in. She screamed and her thirteen-year-old brother ran to the rescue. He pulled her away and her leg was just a bloody stump."

Suddenly, we were at the spot. The water, however, was down from the day before, leaving yesterday's eggs exposed to the sun, and the gar were out deeper, rippling on the surface.

I snuck out with my net, just in time to see a gar tail rise. It slapped the water, and they all shot off.

We ended up chasing a bunch of retarded ducks on the shore, trying to get them with my special gar net. They waddled and quacked while we stumbled after. Kevin went for one, conked it on the head, and it went bumbling around like a drunken uncle.

It's a pathetic sight when grown men fail to get a gar.

Col. J. G. Burr of Texas was the Adolf Hitler of garfish. He was the director of research of the Game Fish and Oyster Commission in Austin in the '30s, where he tried his damnedest to destroy gar through electrocution, virtually sending thousands to the chair.

Colonel Burr's preferred method of execution was stringing a power line across the bottom of a body of water, then dragging buoys connected to ground wires across the surface. He'd send four hundred volts through the power line, and the fish within range would float to the surface, either knocked out or dead.

This shocking behavior on the part of the colonel was encouraged by various bureaus of research and conservation that publicly called for inventors "to devise methods for Gar control, since it is clear that this species is a real menace to many forms of fish and other wild life."

The colonel went on to construct a special boat meant for the mass massacre of gars: the *Electrical Gar Destroyer*. It was an eight-by-sixteen-foot "barge" rigged with a two-hundred-volt generator and an electric net that zapped the fish and scooped them up. A bright red floodlight on the bow then blinded the gar so the colonel could brain them.

On the maiden voyage of the *Electrical Gar Destroyer*, Burr succeeded in wiping out seventy-five alligator gar and one thousand turtles. After that, he went up and down bayous and canals ridding Texas of garfish, even making excursions into salt water to get gar that had fled the threat of his almighty net.

Mr. J. G. McGee of New Mexico then took a hint from the colonel and rigged up something similar in the Pecos River in Roswell. He went to dams where gar had gathered and shocked them to death. Others followed suit, and soon, tons of garfish were floating belly up across the desert Southwest.

Meanwhile, Colonel Burr compiled all sorts of data on killing gar at various depths with various voltages in different degrees of salinity during different months of the summer. He exterminated millions, making a great dent in the American garfish population.

Following a massive gar kill in Lake Caddo, this is what the great sportsman Colonel Burr had to say: "I saw one immense Gar, which seemed to be 7 feet long, spring entirely out of the water 30 feet away. His jump was at an angle of 45 degrees and I am sure he felt the current. This jumping of the Gars, whether they went into the net or not, produced a thrill which can not be found in any other kind of fishing."

Contrary to claims that gar flesh isn't fit for a dog, there doesn't seem to be a shortage of gar meat being sold in the South. I've seen steaks and filets at rinky-dink stores and gas stations all over Louisiana.

In *Fishing Gear Online* there's an article entitled "Gar in the Pan." The author, Keith "Catfish" Sutton, writes:

Actually, gars are rather tasty, a fact that becomes obvious when you learn of the hundreds of thousands of pounds of gar meat being sold each year at Mom-and-Pop fish markets throughout the country. On a recent visit to a south Arkansas fish market, I watched as the proprietor sold hundreds of pounds of gar meat in three hours, at $3 a pound. Catfish fillets, selling for $2.50 per pound, were hardly touched by the customers. . . . "I can't get enough gars to meet the demand," the proprietor told me. "Once folks try it and find out how good it really is, they come back wanting more. The fish are difficult to dress, but the meat cooks up white and flaky, and tastes as good as any fish you ever put in your mouth."

Sutton goes on to tell about how he ate a freshly cut steak from a 190-pound gar, and how he was impressed with it. He compares the taste to crappie, before offering up this poem by W. P. Meyer:

My pan at home it has been greased
For gar he is a tasty beast
I shall invite the local priest
To join me in this garish feast.

Whether the second to the last word in the poem is missing an "f," I can't say, but I can say what follows in the article: step-by-step instructions on how to clean garfish. Basically, this is how it's done:

First, cut off the head and tail with an axe, leaving a big long tube of food. Second, use tin snips to split the bony hide open. Third, peel the meat back from the armor using gloves to protect your fingers. After that, filet the meat along the backbone, then cut into smaller pieces.

Sutton then lists some recipes, including gar stew, gar cakes, stir-fried gar, gar boulettes, and garfish Mississippi. These recipes and others can be found online with a simple Google search.

After all that gar study, I couldn't be held back. So I took off for the Gaspergou Bayou Oil and Gas Fields, where it's said the largest ancient gar in the state still seethe beneath the surface—some of them close to a century old. I was armed with a canoe full of milk jugs with steel guitar strings strung to treble hooks meant for lingcod up in Puget Sound, a bag of rancid turkey necks, two gas cans filled with chum, five cans of dog food, and my father's Luger captured off a Nazi soldier.

I also had one bearded Bulgarian with me, Plamen Arnoudov. Last time I took him fishing, he hooked an endangered paddlefish, and I beat it to death with a hammer. We ate shovelnose for a week—which, of course, is illegal in Louisiana.

But then again, so is fishing without a license—which we intended to do, like almost every single Cajun does. And nobody tells Cajuns not to eat what they catch—that's what they've been doing since the 1600s, hunting and trapping and living off the land. So why should graduate students be any different? Just because the ancestors of Cajuns got abducted from Canada and dumped in a swamp, prompting Longfellow to write some poem about a tree, does that give them more of a right to fish for free? I don't think so.

It didn't really matter, though, because the place we were going was posted "OFF LIMITS." Gaspergou is owned by Texaco, who ran a big old petrochemical processing plant out on a platform until just a few years ago when the state shut them down. Supposedly, they'd been dumping something that couldn't be mentioned in the papers, and now the platform was abandoned.

Anyhow, we snuck through the cypresses. For miles and miles, great horned owls stared down at us while egrets nested all around. There were alligators lying on logs, and copperheads winding through the duckweed. And when we got to the platform, there were vultures perched on giant pipes overgrown with poison ivy. But from a hundred yards away, we could see the surface rippling.

We stayed where we were, baited up our floats, and tossed them out. The wind was with us, blowing toward the platform. Soon, twenty jugs were making their way toward the gar swirls, each of them dangling a big, honking turkey neck.

Then we broke out the chum. I'd bought a case of slicker (freshwater mullet) at a place called Breaux's in Henderson (one box, one dollar), then ground them up in the food processor until they became an oily purée—which I put outside for three days in the sun. When the neighbors started complaining about the stench, I poured the concoction into the gas cans.

So Plamen and I, we poured the stinking soup in the swamp. A reeking brown puddle began following the jugs, and that's when I saw a long, armored back vanish. It was half the size of my canoe!

Drifting closer, we made some bait bombs by pounding holes in the Alpo cans, then hurled them out to smolder under water and get the gars all up in a lather.

We waited. Suddenly a milk jug went under, then reappeared ten feet later. Then another one went down. Then another. The garfish were going nuts over there. We waited until all twenty were bobbing and bopping around the platform, then paddled over and pulled one up.

It had a five-foot gar on it, splashing around in a manic frenzy. There was no way we were going to get it in the boat without tipping over, so I leveled the Luger between its eyes and blasted a hole through its head.

Then we saw the incredible. Its pals began attacking it, swarming it, right beneath us. We could see gar backs passing eight feet long, sometimes longer. They were ripping their fallen comrade to shreds and thrashing on the surface, roiling red with blood.

We gripped the canoe and held on. The buzzards above were screeching like the damned. A couple of times the canoe almost flipped—and we knew what would happen if we went into the drink. But suddenly the ruckus ceased.

Under the platform, we saw nineteen milk jugs on the run. Something had spooked them. Something that made a tremendous splash behind us, causing us to swivel and see a gar so ginormous that I'd lose all credibility as a garfish aficionado if I tried to describe the size of it. I will only say that some of those old books weren't so far off, and that its entire chromy backside was cutting across the swamp, coming our way.

The next thing we knew, we were kicking up a rooster tail and paddling like lunatics. Our only thought was to make it to the Spanish moss and get up in those trees—which we did.

And from that moment on, I no longer felt the burning urge to get a garfish.

2

In Search of Massive Missouri Gar

COMING FROM KIRKSVILLE in northern Missouri, I was blasting down to the Bootheel in my station wagon to check out some supersized taxidermied gar, as well some humans who also had some fish tales to tell. Having researched gar for years, and having received e-mails and JPEGs from gar-nuts all over the world (due to an essay published on the Internet), I had a burning case of Gar Fever, so had struck out in spite of the wintry weather—which was supposed to be over now that it was April.

Shooting south on I-55, the sky growing gray with overcast, I kept the pedal to the metal and watched the rocky landscape dwindle. After the Ozarks, the land became flat and crisscrossed by canals from the Little River Drainage System. Between 1914 and 1928, more cubic yards of earth had been moved here than in the construction of the Panama Canal. This ambitious engineering project had been all about irrigation, and had made agriculture possible in the region. Still, all those levees and ditches had restructured the sensitive spawning grounds of the now-extirpated alligator gar, which requires vast floodplains with sustained water levels in order to reproduce.

Then a freak blizzard hit. It came blowing out of nowhere and started dumping horizontal snow. I could hardly see two car lengths ahead, and the Interstate was turning to slush. Within twenty minutes, everything was white and everyone around me was trying to keep their tires in the icy ruts, but no one was slowing down. We were all doing at least seventy-five, and I was passing in the fast lane.

That's when the car in front of me slid toward the shoulder and the driver overcompensated, cranking the wheel toward the oncoming lane. The car went into a furious spin, and I knew that if I tried to avoid it, I'd end up flipping in the ditch. So as it came spinning at me like a steel tornado, I drove straight toward its vortex and braced for impact.

For a split-second, I was in the eye of the hurricane, and in that split-second, I must've been parallel enough to the whirling car to shoot on through, somehow emerging unscathed. In the rear-view mirror, though, I could see the car still spinning. It smacked the guardrail, bounced off, and slid to a halt. Other cars were slowing down to help, but it didn't make sense for me to stop because I had Jumbo Gar to meet!

Still, I slowed it down to forty-five while my heart jackhammered in my chest. Then, getting off on State Highway 164, I headed west through the shifting drifts and saw some ducks just standing in a snowy field, powder piling up on them. They weren't even trying to find any cover, so I figured they were just as confused as me since it still wasn't clear to me why I was risking my life to look at some stuffed fish and hear some stories. If my wife had been with me, I'm sure we would've turned back a hundred miles ago, or at least pulled over and waited for better conditions.

But I finally made it to the little town of Hornersville on the border of Arkansas and stopped at the gas station. This is where Barry McFarland had told me to meet him when I called last week. I'd seen him in the *Daily Dunklin Democrat* standing next to a mongo mummified alligator gar, and had found his number through directory assistance. He told me to come on down.

When I walked in, Barry was behind the counter. He was wearing a mechanic's outfit and whittling a duck call. In fact, there was a whole glass case full of these award-winning hand-carved suckers, which seemed to be his business on the side.

"You drove through that?" he asked with a shake of his head, and then he shook it some more. Apparently, weather like this wasn't very common in these here parts, and only fools went out on days like this.

Barry, however, had a high-up truck, so a few minutes later we were in it and four-wheel driving to the Duck Club. We got there, went on in, and there it was: all 228 pounds of it, eight feet three inches long.

"It got run over in 1957," Barry explained.

Like many a manatee down in Florida that bit it due to direct contact with a boat, a prop had killed this lunker, which was no doubt one of the last massive gars in Missouri. It had survived the settlers, the mass draining of the southeast corner of the state, but it hadn't been able to escape the machinery of the ever-expanding human world, which is why gator gar are now gone from Missouri when there used to be thousands swimming in the cypressy swamps.

Anyway, I took some pictures, got back on the snowy road, and fishtailed my way up to Kennett. There was a six-foot-six-inch gar there, mounted in the Dunklin County Museum. I'd talked to the museum chair, Sandra Brown, on the phone about this 126-pounder, and she told me it was a hit with the kids. She also told me to come on down.

But, since I lost some time due to the weather and was getting hungry, I set my sights on New Hamburg, where Schindler's Tavern boasted a famous baloney burger, as well as a whopping nine-foot gar displayed above the bar.

Sliding and swerving up Highway 25, I made it to Dexter, the home of Don Jones, who I'd been corresponding with through the e-mail about a seven-foot-ten-inch monster-gar he had shot near Caruthersville in 1960. Don had written me a detailed story about how his father had owned land adjacent to the Mississippi, which had been cleared for farming in the '50s. When Don was fifteen years old, the spring floods made it impossible to till, so his father decided they'd go out on their wooden boat and do some gigging.

That's when two enormous gar showed up, causing a disturbance on the surface. They were flinging driftwood all around, which meant they were spawning. Don and his father tried to get them, but they couldn't get their pitchforks to penetrate the armored scales.

This massive alligator gar hangs on a wall at the Duck Club in Hornersville, Missouri. The eight-foot-three-inch gar, which weighed 228 pounds, died after being hit by a boat prop in 1957. Photo by Mark Spitzer.

Don's father eventually gave up, but Don didn't. He went back for his deer rifle, then went out there again. He shot the smaller one and it started to sink, but he stuck his gig in and hooked it in the bullet hole. Don ended up holding the gig in one hand while the gar thrashed madly, and paddling with the other hand toward shore, where once again he shot the gar—this time in the head.

An old hermit called Gabby, who happened to be hunting rabbits at the time, came along and helped Don load it into the back of a rickety pickup. Don then drove to the bale scales at the cotton gin. The gar weighed 180 pounds and was almost eight feet long. A crowd gathered. A photographer came and took a picture, which was accompanied by a write-up in the local paper that told how the big one got away.

Don was a bit worried about the game warden because he wasn't sure if shooting gar was legal. He never got in trouble, but I felt a sense of regret in his e-mails. He was proud of his catch, but it felt to me that he knew that fish was one of the last big gar in the state, and he had played a hand in its demise.

Back then, however, America was deep in a nationwide campaign to eradicate gar, which left countless cadavers rotting on the river shores. Basically, government-sponsored propaganda from the 1920s and '30s had demonized gar as useless trash fish that attacked humans and ate into gamefish populations. Lacking scientific knowledge on the species, conservation departments across the country reacted to stereotypes based on the gar's fierce appearance and spent decades encouraging their extermination. Plus, the scientists and naturalists who weighed in on the dialogue (often describing gar as "worthless") didn't do much to help their reputation.

If anyone's to blame, though, for spreading mis-fish-information, it was the media. Especially the anonymous journalist who wrote an alarmist article in a 1922 issue of the *Times-Picayune* of New Orleans, which relied on a laundry list of undocumented innuendo to conclude that gar destroy "millions of food fishes, and the cause of conservation would be advanced by his destruction."

But that wasn't all gar had to contend with. There was overfishing, bowhunting, sportfishing, and the harvesting of huge gar, in general, through whatever means possible. Their destruction was culturally and socially sanctioned, and nobody cared enough to defend them.

Evidence, however, has since been gathered that gar feed mainly on whatever is most abundant in their habitats, which are usually crustaceans or members of the sucker and minnow families. Research has also concluded that gar are advantageous to maintaining equilibrium in ecosystems. And

A fifteen-year-old Don Jones stands beside the almost-eight-foot-long gar he shot in 1960 near Caruthersville, Missouri. Photo courtesy of Don Jones.

for all the stories about swimmers getting chomped on by gore-crazed gar, there's not one verified account in existence of a garfish ever attacking a human.

It's a tradition, of course, to distort the facts when it comes to fish, but even more so when it comes to gigantic alligator gar—as in the story of the legendary lunker in Schindler's Tavern, where I found myself braving the blizzard to get to. The story goes that after being pulled from a ditch by Martin Bisher and his horse in 1916, the gar was hauled into town on the back of a wagon and the whole town had a feast.

I'd been in contact with Martin's grandson Leon, whose uncle had inherited that big stuffed gar. Leon used to sit on it when he went to visit. That gar was left to the Schindlers when Leon's uncle passed away.

Since then, the tavern has gone through several owners. It has also gone through several regional reporters who made the claim that this 180-pounder was "nine feet long." But when I parked my car and walked in, I could immediately see that it was only six-foot-something, yellowed by years of cigarette smoke, and grinning down at me as if to say, "Ha, fooled ya!"

That's what happens, though: the bigger the fish, the bigger its myths. So I ordered a baloney burger and a beer and talked to the bartender. He let me get up on the counter and take a few pictures and measure the gar. It was six-foot-nine. Then I ate my baloney burger, and it's "deliciousness" was just as embellished as the fish.

That night I slept in my sleeping bag in the back of the station wagon, parked between two semis at a truck stop. It was cold and hard and I didn't get much sleep, but in the morning I went and got some coffee, then drove into Cape Girardeau to meet with Christopher Kennedy, a fisheries biologist for the Missouri Department of Conservation. Kennedy was trying to reintroduce alligator gar into the Mingo Wildlife Refuge to the west, a swampy labyrinth still inhabited by longnose, shortnose and spotted gar.

It was a Saturday and Kennedy didn't have to come into the office, but as he told me as we shook hands, "I'm glad to meet anyone who wants to talk gar."

Like me, Kennedy grew up fascinated by this mysterious fish, which he used to catch with his father. His father, however, used to break off their beaks and throw them back, which wasn't (and still isn't) too uncommon a practice for those who were raised to detest the species. And this always bummed Kennedy out.

This is part of the reason he studied gar, became a specialist in gar, and is now gar expert and gar advocate. So we had a lot to talk about:

"Nine-foot" gar in Schindler's Tavern, New Hamburg, Missouri. Photo by Mark Spitzer.

decades of gar slander and sloppy science, garfishing techniques, gar diets, gar studies, and, of course, the 115-pound, six-foot-four alligator gar mounted in the building next door.

Kennedy asked me if I wanted to see it, but I declined. I knew the story: It was shot with a bow and arrow by David Smith in 2001 and was presently the state record because—like most states where larger gar have been taken—nobody thought they were worth documenting until later in the twentieth century. Or, in the case of Missouri, the twenty-first century.

The thing is, at the turn of the millennium, gator gar were believed to be extinct in Missouri. Until, that is, this one was shot in the Diversion Channel south of Cape Girardeau. And just as the breaking off of their beaks never sat quite right with Kennedy, the killing of this magnificent fish (which could be anywhere from twenty-five to eighty years old), didn't sit quite right with me.

So we focused on the Alligator Gar Reintroduction Project, which I had come to interview Kennedy about. He had received approval to stock twenty radio-tagged twenty-five-inchers, and, if all went according to plan, he'd get them in the water this summer and track their movements to gather data on their ranges.

"These guys were meant to be here," Kennedy explained. "The system was designed for them."

But reintroduction of any fanged creature (as in the case of the timber wolf or grizzly bear) is always a touchy process. There are misconceptions that need to be addressed so that misunderstandings are not repeated. Hence, Kennedy had plans for what he termed "re-education." In addition to brochures and posters to spread awareness, the idea was for the Department of Conservation to work with The Friends of Mingo and other environmental groups to inform citizens through a series of public meetings.

"We've also started to develop activities for elementary through high school students," Kennedy said, "to help explain the alligator gar's role in the ecosystem."

Asked if the idea was to restock gar for sportfishing, Kennedy replied, "Our main objective is for the ecology of the system . . . but I'd love to catch one myself."

As to whether these gar will be protected, Kennedy responded that it will take two or more years to get regulations in place. Still, anglers can be asked to help protect alligator gar, even though it's unlikely anyone will encounter them within the first few years, since Mingo Swamp is not highly accessible. "You'd have to paddle back there or use a trolling motor," Kennedy said, "and then you can only go back there at certain times of the year." As for bowhunting, projectile weapons have been banned in the refuge.

Kennedy told me that he hoped to stock alligator gar every year to bring their numbers up. He believed the stock would find its way down to Arkansas, but because "there's enough research to speculate that they have [homing] characteristics," he was pretty sure they'd return, as do salmon.

I asked Kennedy what these gar will feed on, and he replied that there's no need to stock feeder populations, because there's "plenty of food in the system to support them . . . they're going to be looking for fish species that also like the open-water habitat . . . we're talking shad, buffalo, carp."

Kennedy stated that big gar want "the biggest bang for their buck," so will therefore "focus on larger-prey species," especially shad, which can get a foot long and are abundant in Mingo. "And when they get that long," Kennedy added, "there's nothing else in there that's going to feed on them." He also predicted that when the gar stock grow large enough to start eating the larger shad, "you'll see less bigger shad and more smaller shad . . . [which] will actually help the gamefish populations."

Kennedy then got down to the meat of the matter (at least for me), by suggesting that this restoration project offers us more than just the opportunity to repopulate the state with a really cool fish. Since big gar tend to feed on big members of the minnow family, he indicated that this project could lead to a partial solution in controlling the highly invasive Asian carp, which are presently reaping destruction in the Mississippi and its tributaries by destroying the nests of indigenous fish. Not only that, but they're creating safety hazards by leaping in front of motorboats and smacking people upside their heads.

This led me to question what I would rather see in the waters of Missouri: a pesky alien carp, or a nine-foot, three-hundred-pound, motherlunker gator gar thrashing and splashing all silver on the surface like some prehistoric fish come back from the past.

And the answer, of course, is obvious.

It then occurred to me that maybe there's a way to market alligator gar as a patriotic fish protecting American waters from ichthyological terrorists that represent one of the last bastions of Communism left on the planet. Still, it seemed pretty obvious that refocusing the hatred people have for gar on another species wouldn't really add to anyone becoming more enlightened, even if this could be a way of getting those dang carp under control.

Anyhow, since Kennedy could see that I wanted to "be good for something" (to quote Thoreau), he invited me to come down later in the summer and go out on an airboat to release alligator gar into Mingo Swamp. I thanked him and hit the road.

The blizzard was gone and the highway was clear. But as things turned out, I lost touch with Kennedy and the gar stock never got released that summer. There was still too much uncertainty, red tape, and residual fear.

A year and a half later, though, I received my monthly copy of the *Missouri Conservationist* and read that Kennedy had released "300 young *kerplunkers* to their native dark waters," where alligator gar "hadn't set fin . . . for more than 30 years."

So now they're back. And hopefully, they'll keep coming back, and keep getting reintroduced.

Meanwhile, my Gar Fever has increased to the point that I've become a gar-fanatic who believes that re-educating people about alligator gar isn't just about taking responsibility for what we've messed up. It's also about whether we have the character to overcome our nature for overcoming nature—something I've never had much faith in, but would love to see breed massive Missouri gar.

3

Gar and Loathing in Texahoma

SINCE HIPPY AND I had Gar Fever, we were totally psyched for seven-footers. We had hired the world-famous gator-gar guide Captain Kirk, so were bombing down through Oklahoma to get ourselves a gar. The plan was to meet up with the legendary Rex Rose in Texas, fish for a day with the captain, then go out the next day on our own. It was early May, Hippy was driving, and my stripy yellow-green canoe was strapped on top of the station wagon.

"Man, we are going to get some monster gar," I said, "then swim with them and skitch a ride to Mexico!"

"Yeah," he replied, "they're going down!"

"We Gotta Bomb It!" I yelled. "We Gotta Make It! It's On!"

"Yeeehaw!" Hippy howled, and kicked it up to sixty-two.

"Come on, Granny!" I shouted at him. "This here's the Interstate! You call this Bombing it!? We got gar to catch!"

Hippy got it up to sixty-six, which was still too slow for me. I had Gar Fever to the max! For the last five years, I'd been studying gar, researching gar, writing gar, dreaming gar, and trying to catch them to no avail. I had Gar OCD! I had Gar Megalomania! And so did Hippy! We were going Gonzo for Gar! Sweating gar, seeing gar, totally focused on some distant gar-point nine hundred miles away and shooting down to Huntsville with fishing licenses and everything to get some massive world-class gar!

"Watch out for the Feds!" I said, eyeing the speedometer. "They're everywhere! And they'll only slow us down!"

"Feds!" Hippy howled, taking his foot off the gas.

"No!" I screamed. "It's the only way to ditch them. They can't see you when you're booking! It's like when the Flash vibrates all his molecules—he becomes invisible!"

"Okay," Hippy said, and punched it up to sixty-eight.

Hippy was my student—or, rather, used to be my grad student. When I came to Missouri four years ago, we immediately clicked and took off fishing. Caught tons of bass and channel cats. Plus, we were big on bullfrogs croaking at night while taking pulls from a whiskey flask.

"C'mon!" I yowled. "Where's that speed!? Where's that passion!?"

"But the Feds," Hippy said, "they've got radars!"

"If you vibrate fast enough, there's no way they can pick you up!" I replied, owing no allegiance whatsoever to the idea of being a role model —or anything responsible. Nope, not when there were gar to catch!

"Garrrr!" Hippy pirated back, and kicked it up to sixty-nine.

He was tall and blond and crazy-haired and dressed in his typical overalls with that big old bushy beard and a pair of stinking sandals—which stunk because his feet stunk. Hippy was living a pungent lifestyle. Not washing had become a political statement among the anarchists he lived with. But to me, his feet just reeked with a funky, stanky noxiousness that came smoking off his fetid toes and went smoldering up into my nose so sweet and thick I could taste it with every breath. And it wasn't getting any better as the day got hotter and hotter.

So the moment we crossed into Texas, I spotted a sign for a public launch and ordered him to take the exit. He did, and we followed a winding road to the lake, passing some truck guys going the other way. We waved at them and they waved back, and then we came to the gate and drove on down to the launch.

"Get out and wash your feet," I told Hippy when we stopped, and handed him some dishwashing soap. He got out all apologetic, while I opened the doors to air the car out.

"And scrub off all that rot and fungus!" I called to Hippy, down at the lake. "And hurry up! Time's a-wastin'!"

Hippy came grinning back to the car, his feet smelling lemony fresh. There was a payphone there, so I dialed up the legendary Rex Rose.

"Hey," I told him, "we're bombing it!"

"Well, you better make it by ten o'clock," he told me, "because that's when they close the state park. I'm in the campground now, setting up camp."

"Okay," I said, "see you soon" and hung up, hopped in, gunned the V6, and shot off before Hippy even shut the door.

But when we got back up to the gate, it was padlocked shut. Those truck guys had locked us in!

"Feds!" Hippy said, looking all around. "The ding dang Feds!"

"We Gotta Cut It!" I replied, and jumped out with two pairs of needle nose pliers and we got to work taking down the barbed wire.

"In Texahoma," I told Hippy as we snipped, "there's nothing lower than a fence-cutter. In fact, they call them 'cutters' down here and hang them from the highest tree!"

"Shoot," Hippy said. "We got to get out of here!"

I jumped back in, Hippy peeled back the cut fence, and I tore up a strip of sod twenty feet long. Then, shooting on through, I skidded to a halt and Hippy dove in through the window.

"Hit It!" he yelled, and we blew out of there, screeching onto the asphalt, leaving one vandalized fence and a violated lawn behind. But at least we ditched the Feds!

And that's what we continued to do. I was blasting back to my muscle-car past and driving like those damn kids who go squealing through my neighborhood—the ones I yell and shake my fist at. But we were driving Harder Faster, because I was raised on *Dukes of Hazzard* and $1.20 gasoline. High school was a study in neutral drops and brake stands and skidding sideways down the street, then going fishy and cranking the wheel and spinning out and torquing out and learning how to crash Chevelles. Meaning I had rowdy, reckless driving skills that I had honed and set aside. Till now! Because we were gripped by Gar Fever and the camp-ground was closing down and the Feds had called in air support—so I put the hammer down.

Police municipality after police municipality, we bombed our way through the vast scrubland all around us. There was no Interstate now, just county road after county road and small towns everywhere. And as we shot along, it started to get dark—which only made it easier to fly right by the sheriff, who was always idling in his car, staring at a hamburger.

Mother of God! I must've screamed past at least a hundred coppers mesmerized by hamburgers!

And so what if they hit the cherries? I'd just ditch them like I used to do back in the days of faux GTOs and beat El Caminos. It had to be done! Up Yours, Feds! We had jumbo gar to catch!

Meanwhile, Hippy was plastered to his seat. He wasn't objecting, but his teeth and eyes were clenched as giant yellow grasshoppers splattered on the windshield.

"Thirty-Five Miles Per Hour!" I yelled, tearing past a speed-limit sign in some one-horse town. "That Means seventy!"

Then punching it up to eighty-five, I swerved around an SUV only going sixty-five. I was all the way over in the oncoming lane and two huge semis were coming our way, but I bore down and shot back onto our side, the fastest temporary assistant professor in Texahoma, USA.

I never drove like this before. My wife will attest to this: I'm the slowest driver on the planet—annoyingly so! But that, of course, is when there aren't gar to catch.

Anyway, it was now nine o'clock and we had a hundred miles to go. As I got back onto the Interstate, Hippy started loosening up, then yucking away like some gangly goofy hillbilly in it for the ride. And, of course, the humongous gar on the other side!

Then kicking it up to ninety-five, I took to the passing lane and started blowing Porsches away. The speedometer rose to ninety-six, ninety-eight, one hundred miles per hour!

"Why not?" I muttered, and pushed it up to 104, 106, 110. Then we made it to the park. It was 9:59 p.m. as we blew past the gate, then coasted into the camping spot and stumbled out on wobbly legs.

The legendary Rex Rose came over and picked me up in a hulking hug. He was like a nitrate-fed Huey P. Long in his Col. Sanders southern duds and ten-gallon safari hat. The campfire was going and he was playing some thump-thump-thumping electronica straight out of some Euro-Nordic disco club.

The legendary Rex Rose had been homeschooled by his father, an eccentric historian who wrote a book on Storyville in New Orleans, that turn-of-the-century red-light district popularized in the Brooke Shields's movie *Pretty Baby*. That's where the legendary Rex Rose grew up and played in the punk band The Rex Pistols, shucking oysters for a job, and living with his wife who blew her head off. After that, he worked with me on the literary journal *Exquisite Corpse*, wrote and published the cult-classic novel *TOAST*, then shot off to be jolly in Portland and live off his inheritance of original Bellocq prints. Now, however, the legendary Rex Rose was lying low in Austin, teaching English to Mongolians and swinging secret deals.

Anyway, we fried up some potatoes with purple onions, threw in some baloney-foam wienies, spiced it up with chili powder, then chowed down and crashed out under the Texahoma stars.

Only to awake at 6:00 a.m. to get ourselves some gator gar! The legendary Rex Rose was already dressed in that double-breasted three-piece suit he somehow managed to keep clean all day out on the muddy river. He was stoking the fire and blasting über-techno at Nature. Squirrels and coons were running for cover. A pileated woodpecker joined in above, pecking like a jackhammer.

We were right on the edge of an alligator lake filled with bass and bream and hyacinth gleaming greenly in the dusk, but we had no time to mess around. We got that cowboy coffee going, slammed it down, and piled into Rex's Volvo. He cranked the wattage all the way up to show us how his woofers could woof—then woofed on through the campground in a flurry of tweets and robot beeps, and we thunka-thunka-thunked into town and got ourselves some low-sodium biscuits n' gravy at the Krogers.

"Man!" I said. "We're going to catch the Big One!"

"Yeah," Hippy added. "Two hundred and fifty pounds!"

"No way," the legendary Rex Rose put in. "Three hundred and sixty-two!"

We'd been waiting years for this, each in our own gar universe. Hippy had grown up in the Ozarks where the longnose sunned on the Gasconade, and the legendary Rex Rose, of course, hailed from the Big Easy, where gangs of roving alligator gar stalked the streets at night. Meaning the three of us each had our own gar histories leading up to the one coming on like the rising sun. The fever was burning!

"We got to meet Captain Kirk," I said, and we hightailed it out of there and met him in the parking lot, where he was waiting with his gartruck and garboat, all fueled up and full of gargear. Captain Kirk was an ex-cop and with his crewcut and no-nonsense attitude exuding, he looked it. Over the last few years he'd gotten a lot of press in angling magazines and cable shows spotlighting gator gar. His name was the most well respected in all of gar-getting, his reputation was international, and in the past eight years, no client had ever caught anything less than a 130-pounder. And since we'd seen pictures, success was garanteed!

In no time at all we were at the launch, where I noticed that something stunk. At first I thought it was Hippy's feet, but then I saw the bloated beast. It was lying by the shore with flies buzzing all around it: a hundred-pound, five-and-a-half-foot fatty.

"Holy crap," I said. "What the heck?"

"Stupid bowhunters!" Captain Kirk growled. "Their daddies taught them to throw them on the shore like that, so that's what they teach their kids. People still think gar are a pest. It's a shame!"

The captain was strictly catch-and-release. He believed in keeping the big ones around—if not for his business, then, at least, because they're pretty dang spectacular and they don't do anyone any harm.

Another thing he told us was that any gar over thirty pounds was always female.

But back to the bloated gar on the shore:

"That's screwed up," I said to Hippy. "I wonder what Ted Nugent would say about people wasting creatures twice their age, then dumping them like dogs to die."

"Wang Dang Sweet Gartang!" Hippy responded, and went into an air-guitar lick of "The Great White Buffalo" riff, until we hopped on into the boat. Captain Kirk fired up the 150-horse, and we shot off.

Downstream, we got to the spot and pulled up on the bank, where the captain started chopping up drum. Then he rigged us up with some extra-large surf-fishing reels on mongo sturdy Ugly Stiks as fat around as broomsticks and directed us where to cast.

"If a gar takes it," he said, "just let her run. If she goes toward the middle of the river then heads downstream, that's a gar. If it heads toward the shore, it's only a stupid turtle."

Immediately, the legendary Rex Rose got a bite. His float started bopping toward shore.

"Stupid!" Captain Kirk addressed the turtle. "Get outta here, ya Stupid!"

That's when my line took off, heading downstream, right down the middle.

"Reel Em In!" Captain Kirk commanded my comrades, and cast off.

The gar was taking line out fast and we were floating after it. Adrenaline was shooting through all my tubeways and my inner-catfisherman was trying to restrain himself from setting the hook. But then the float stopped and the V behind it vanished just like that.

"Stupid!" Captain Kirk yelled at the gar. "Ya dropped it, ya stupid Stupid!"

"Does that happen a lot?" the legendary Rex Rose asked.

"Sometimes when a cold front comes in," the captain replied.

It was nine in the morning and coming up on seventy degrees. For Texas, this was a cold front.

And so the day went on, Captain Kirk taking us from spot to spot—where he'd pull up and call out, "Okay girls, come and get it!"

But they never came and they never got it and we never got a bite after that first hit. Instead, we just listened to Captain Kirk go on about his clients from the Netherlands, Australia, Japan, England, et cetera. And how he's gone fishing for giant catfish on the Mekong. And hooo-weeee, we should of seen that nine-foot-six-inch lunker-gar he caught back in '82!

And as we waited for gar, we saw them jumping all around us. Yep, as the heat picked up, so did their action, till the river was aboil with five-, six-, seven-foot gar, breaching like behemoths, flashing for a split-second, then disappearing like the Mythic Big One.

At one point I saw one as fat around as a trash can and just about the same color, but then it twisted in the sky and I saw its belly gleaming whitely.

"C'mon Stupids!" Captain Kirk kept saying. "Stupid Stupids! C'mon!"

But the gar weren't the only "stupids" in the works that day. For instance, "that stupid Catfish Sutton" came up a couple of times. He was a fish writer whose work I knew, and had even swapped fish books with.

"That Stupid's such a Stupid!" Captain Kirk said. "He writes all these articles on alligator gar, sells 'em to all these glossy magazines, but he's never caught one! 'Where'd you get your information?' I asked him, and he said, 'The Internet.' So I told him to his face, right there on the phone, that he's a Stupid! Because you can't go and write about gator gar if you've never caught one! What a Stupid!"

I didn't mention, of course, that I was in the same boat as Catfish Sutton, so was therefore a Stupid, too—at least in the eyes of the captain.

So we waited and waited and waited all day, and watched the gar slapping and slapping and slapping all day. They were teasing us, laughing at us, making us feel impotent. Because there they were—thirty, twenty, ten feet away—and we couldn't do anything accept drop our jaws every time they flashed their fins.

"C'mon Stupids!" Captain Kirk yelled, kicking back on his lawn chair on the bow. "We'll wait it out till midnight if we gotta. C'mon, Stupids!"

Then Kirk decided to tease Hippy, since he heard about how I made him wash his feet. Then after that, the captain started ribbing the legendary Rex Rose for snarling up a bait-casting reel. That went on for almost an hour.

By 8:00 p.m. we were all Starvin Marvins. Not only that, but since any idiot could see that the gar weren't biting, we knew it wasn't very likely that they'd get hungry in the next four hours. So we packed it up and went back to the launch.

Where I went to check on that murtilated gar. Its mouth was frozen open, its eyes were bulging hideously, it was way more bloated than earlier that day, and a bunch of guts had erupted from a rupture underneath its neck. There was also a hole in the center of its head writhing with a squiggling sludge of maggot porridge.

"Christ," Hippy said.

"P.U.," I replied.

"Let's go get some non-hydrogenated food items," the legendary Rex Rose put in.

And so we did. And guess what? After zero grams of trans-fat, the liquor stores were all closed up, so we couldn't even get any bourbon to help us forget that we'd just paid $183 each to catch a gar we never caught.

Stupids!

In the morning, the legendary Rex Rose had to techno back to Austin, so Hippy and I went back to the launch where the slaughtered gar was kicking out a toxic cloud of gagging stomach-wrenching gases that everybody within the radius of a football field had to huff, thanks to the stewardship of the good ol' Texas bowhunting boys.

Still, we got the canoe loaded up, took off upstream, went around a bend and found a beach with a slow-turning eddy, gars flopping everywhere. This was the spot, so we broke out our stuff—like my special gar-rod I'd bought at a pawn shop up in Missouri. It was short and stout and as thick around as a corndog, probably meant for paddlefish snagging. It had an extra large bait-casting reel strung with one-hundred-pound test and a two-hundred-forty-pound custom muskie leader from Wisconsin (and muskies don't even get that big). Hippy, on the other hand, had a seven-foot catfishing rod rigged with sixty-five-pound test and another muskie leader.

So we set our poles up on the beach, then settled in. For hours, the gar danced across our stage while we sat there in the blazing rays. They just weren't taking our bait, which was frozen shrimp and shad.

Eventually, we paddled out and set some drop-lines along the bank, then hotfooted it back to the beach, where we proceeded to roast some more in the sun—which was one intense ball of flaming hydrogen baking us alive.

"Forget this," I told Hippy, "let's go for a swim."

"Swim," in this case, meant stripping down and sitting in the water up to our necks, while the gar swam circles around us. If one attacked, we figured it would be up to the other to haul his mangled pal to shore. Not for the purpose of saving his life, but so the other guy could get a gar. That's why the jack handle from my car was lying on the sand. But wouldntchya know it? No gargantugar attacked that day.

Then it was time to pack it up and drift back to the launch, where the putrid gar had become a totally rank dirty bomb of super-noxious chemical warfare, filling the world with poison vapors. It was a good thing we didn't eat any lunch.

Back in the car, I put the pedal down, burning up that three-dollar gas like no tomorrow. We had to get away from that rotting gar, so, again, I was driving eighty-five.

Not ninety, though, because our Gar Fever was totally gone, making for a different ride. With no gar upon the horizon, life was suddenly totally pointless. Ahead, there was nothing but a vast void of country music and no NPR for eight hundred miles.

A few days later, I was back in Kirksville, when I decided to go fishing on the Chariton, which is our humble little Midwestern river. And who should I see when I'm cutting through town, but Hippy, walking the other way.

"I'm going fishing," I yelled to him. "Want to come along?"

"Yeah!" he said, and hopped on in. His gear was still in my car, so we took off.

Twenty minutes later, we were ducking under the poison ivy, which was already red and angry and choleric. Then following the trail down to the bank, we were casting out our night crawlers and trying to act like we weren't losers for failing to get a gar.

"It's like having sex," I told Hippy, referring back to our conversation with Captain Kirk regarding Catfish Sutton. "You can't say anything about it if you've never done it."

"What a pile of crap that is," Hippy said, and suddenly his line took off, straight and fast, no holding back.

"Set it!" I yelled, and Hippy cranked back. It caught. No doubt, a flathead or channel cat.

But nope! It was a two-foot-long silvery gar! And Hippy was cheering—because we never had to go to Texas, and we never needed all that gear, and we never needed Captain Kirk to get a gar—because all we needed was a worm!

So I was jumping up and down. Because Hippy was me, losing my garginity. I mean, that's what I was seeing, that's what I was feeling: I was reeling in that gar!

Then I grabbed it, just like any fish, and held it up—all two whopping pounds of it. Granted, it was no three-hundred-pound, muskrat-munching gator gar that had been lurking in the murk for eighty years—but that didn't matter.

What mattered was that the story now had an honest ending in which a simple little shortnose was enough to make it all worthwhile.

4

Gator vs. Gar

A History of Misinformation

DUE TO ITS FOUNDATION in the oral tradition, the genre of the fish story is automatically suspect. But when it comes to gar, I started to notice a lot more fishy information in the mix—like bias in the early science, and the media exaggerating the danger factor. And as I stepped up my study of the history and folklore of this fish, while still steeped deep in Gar Fever, I began to notice a certain chain of completely unfounded rumors.

So I dove into my steadily growing garchives, looking for some answers, especially in regard to the classic question of who would whoop who: an alligator or an alligator gar? Which, for some reason, keeps getting addressed in the body of literature existing on gar. This age-old scenario, of course, has roots in the juvenile question of whether a lion can lick a tiger, and it's reflected in our fascination with movies such as *Godzilla vs. King Kong*, *Freddy vs. Jason*, and *Alien vs. Predator*.

Basically, what I discovered was that reports of alligators fighting with alligator gars can be traced back to 1820, when a second-hand report on some gator-on-gar action was popularized by Constantine Rafinesque, for whom the shortnose gar *(Lepisosteus platostomus Rafinesque)* was named. Rafinesque wrote *Ichthyologia Ohiensis: Or Natural History of the Fishes Inhabiting the River Ohio and Its Tributary Streams,* and from the first page on, warning flags pop up. Because when an author's byline reads "Professor of Botany and Natural History in Transylvania University, Author of the Analysis of Nature, &c. &c. Member of the Literary and Philosophical Society of New-York, the Historical Society of New-York, the Lyceum of Natural History of New York, the Academy of Natural Sciences of Philadelphia, the American Antiquarian Society, the Royal Institute of Natural

Sciences of Naples, the Italian Society of Arts and Sciences, the Medical Societies of Lexington and Cincinnati, & c. & c.," readers are naturally left with the impression that the author's intention is to convince his readership of his great authority through association with organizations rather than actual research.

Plus, a certain caution is also recommended when referring to any ichthyological text written by a botanist whose formal training is not as evident as his highly boastable accolades. The word "doctor" does not appear anywhere in the byline above, nor does any degree from any institution that indicates a specialization in the life sciences—a fact that's illuminated even more in the aggressive and elitist disclaimer that follows: *"The art of seeing well, or of noticing and distinguishing with accuracy the objects which we perceive, is a high faculty of the mind, unfolded in few individuals, and despised by those who can neither acquire it, nor appreciate its results."*

Still, any early taxonomy, whether it be flawed or not, is valuable if it contributes to a dialogue that invites more analysis. If a text offers information to refute, so much the better for the scientific method, which puts theories to the test and proves them to be relevant if they cannot be disproved.

To make a vast generalization, the nineteenth century was a bumbling era for science, which was slowly emerging from the coercion of the church. It had only been a few centuries since stating that the world was round had been considered heresy, chemists had recently been alchemists, and Darwin's take on evolution wasn't even a concept until the 1850s. It took most of the nineteenth century for surgeons to learn to wash their hands before operating and delivering babies. Meanwhile, half of all new mothers in Europe were dying from bacterial infections.

The 1800s was also a time when our most celebrated American naturalist, Henry David Thoreau, was using *Walden* to spread the lie that "horned pout . . . are dull and blundering fellows . . . [that] will take any kind of bait, from an angleworm to a piece of tomato can." And just as Thoreau's utter malarkey was appropriated and repeated by other writers, establishing the popular misnomer that bullheads eat tin cans, Rafinesque's hearsay regarding gar received similar attention.

So what did Rafinesque write and publish concerning this battle of the titans? Here are his exact words: "Mr. John D. Clifford told me that he saw [a gar] . . . fight with an alligator five feet long and succeed in devouring him, after cutting him in two in its powerful jaws."

This fish story became something like an urban legend, reappearing in the works of other writers throughout the following decades. Edward R.

Ricciuti, for instance, continued the gator-vs.-gar tradition by paraphrasing similar word-of-mouth information in his book *Killers of the Seas*. He wrote that Charles Haskins Townsend, "the New York Aquarium authority, once quoted fishermen from the area of Lake Charles, Louisiana, as saying that alligator gars and American alligators sometimes fight, with the alligators usually victors over their namesakes." Ricciuti then added, "That may be true, as alligators habitually prey on smaller species of gar,—but should an alligator engage an alligator gar of comparable size in combat, the struggle probably would be a nip-and-tuck affair."

So here's where sloppy scholarship confuses things even more: Ricciuti stated that Townsend called "the alligator gar the freshwater counterpart of the shark, [and] wrote in 1920 of receiving a letter from a man who was mauled by a giant gar while bathing in a Louisiana lake." Ricciuti, however, confused two very different garticles. The one comparing gars to sharks was actually published in 1922 by an unknown author in New Orleans's *Times-Picayune*. Furthermore, Steve Johnson, archivist of the Bronx Zoo library, cannot confirm that Townsend ever wrote this piece, since it does not appear in the cumulative staff bibliography of the Wildlife Conservation Society. Plus, the *Times-Picayune* article mentions a bathing barber being attacked by a ten-foot gar, but this information is not presented as being gleaned from a letter.

Still, Townsend did write an article titled "Notes on the Alligator Gar" (published in a 1928 issue of the *Bulletin of the New York Zoological Society*), which referred to two letters. The first was from Dr. J. L. Wortman and had to do with the habits of gar, but it mentions nothing concerning gar attacks. The second was from Dr. Clark Wissler of the American Museum of Natural History, and it addressed an entirely different matter (gar scales as arrowheads), while relying on information from another writer, this one from 1768.

But back to Rafinesque, the original twister of garfish misinformation, who is easily discredited. First of all, his study claims "that there are more than ten specie of these fishes in the United States," when we now know there couldn't have been more than four in the Ohio River system. Listing more species than actually exist, though, was a specialty of Rafinesque, who, according to *The Kentucky Encyclopedia* (1992), is "Best known for remarkable fecundity in divising [sic] scientific names." As *Appleton's Cyclopedia of American Biography* (1889) observes: "The number of genera and species that he introduced into his works produced great confusion. A gradual deterioration is found in Rafinesque's botanical writings from 1819 till 1830, when the passion for establishing new genera and species seems to have become a monomania with him . . . It is said that he wrote a paper describing 'twelve new species of thunder and lightning.'"

Secondly, Rafinesque's listing of the gar subspecies (which he names willy-nilly, citing his own articles) also raises quite a few questions. He starts out with the "Duckbill Garfish," which "bears the names of "Gar, Garfish, Alligator Gar, Alligator Garfish, Jack or Gar Pike." Then comes his description of the "White Garfish," which "reaches the length of six feet, and is often called Garpike or Pike-gar." The "Ohio Gar" (another six-footer) is listed next, so is no doubt an alligator gar as well. Two gar species later we get to the category of "Alligator Garfish," which "reaches the length of eight to twelve feet." The fish following this is listed as a "Diamond Fish" and is noted as having *"Stony scales"* and being related "to the same family." Then comes the "Devil-Jack Diamond-Fish" (also noted for its ganoidy scale pattern), in which Rafinesque bases his notations upon "the description and figure given me by Mr. Audubon;" adding that "Its length is from 4 to 10 feet. One was caught which weighed 400lbs."

Consequently, we get at least six different possibilities for the alligator gar, all listed as separate fish, with much of Rafinesque's information coming from cronies. Either that, or from musing over the dead heads of cadaver-less gar given to him for his study, in which inferences were made on missing bodies and habits were established based on guesswork.

Hence, Rafinesque pioneered "gar scholarship" before the standards for modern taxonomy even became the norm—the result being a type of casual biology based on the unsubstantiated data of a highly ambitious, semi-scientific kook who fancied himself a "poet-philologist."

It should also be noted that Rafinesque had an active interest in conspiracy. Back in 1836 he claimed to have translated a document titled *The Walam Olum,* which was supposedly written by the Lenape (or Delaware) Indians. However, David Oestreicher, a leading authority on these tribes, concluded that the manuscript was written in English first and translated into Lenape later. Consequently, Oestreicher exposed Rafinesque's work on *The Walam Olum* as a hoax inspired by Joseph Smith's latter-day "translation" of *The Book of Mormon* from 1832, which Rafinesque was more than just familiar with. Having researched Smith's work in depth and having publicly denounced it as a forgery, Rafinesque apparently followed suit, producing some apocryphal literature of his own—which was considered authentic for 160 years. According to Oestreicher, Rafinesque did this "out of a desire for fame and recognition."

So that's how the sham scientist who fabricated a Native American creation legend essentially set the stage for all those who followed in what

I term "garology," an ambiguous discipline founded almost entirely on speculation, distortion, and highly unfounded claims. And when science goes unchecked like this, it's not too uncommon (especially in the age of "phrenology") for xenophobic biases to get marketed as fact.

The result of such prejudicial erudition, of course, is even more of the same. For example, in the 1920 edition of *The Fishes of Illinois*, Stephen Alfred Forbes and Robert Earl Richardson continue the unchallenged tradition of stigmatizing gar by reaffirming that this fish is: "a wholly worthless and destructive nuisance in its relations to mankind. It is the enemy of practically all the other fishes in our waters, and so far as it eats anything but fishes, it subtracts from the food supply of the more valuable kinds. It has, in fact all the vices and none of the virtues of a predaceous fish. . . . and by most their destruction is rightly sought."

This general contempt for gar eventually established itself in the mainstream press and, in a FOX News kind of way, influenced other publications to adopt a similar perspective. Thus, we get *Sports Afield* making

Gator vs. Gar. It's easy to see who won this battle in the Florida Everglades. Photo courtesy of Rustin Gooden.

this claim in 1940: "Having no commercial value and generally considered unworthy of conquest by sportsmen, these terrible fresh water wolves live practically unmolested from birth to their natural death . . . their flesh is looked upon with considerable disdain. . . . [and] those countless fishermen who spend days on end in the pursuit of trout, bass, and the other game scrappers, would do well by devoting a fraction of this time to the destruction of the gars."

Still, there is one advantage to a field of study so heavily based on taste: The already shot credibility of its scholarly history makes it appropriate for me to offer my own analysis and pass it off as just as valid. So here it is, derived from observing my own pet gar and others in the marshes:

Whereas gar are generally wary of creatures their own size or larger, and whereas they usually shy away from anything big enough to do them harm, they will defend themselves if suddenly frightened. When this happens, though, and if it comes to blows, it's always more likely that the victor will be the one with the advantage of forelegs and claws.

As Nathaniel Goddard explains in his biological portrait of *Lepisosteidae Atractosteus Spatula*, once gar "reach a size of about 3 feet (1 m) their only natural predator [is] . . . an American alligator." So take that, Rafinesque, for the silly debate you sparked, and all the misinformation it ultimately spawned.

5

The Existential Fish-Life Crisis

(or How I Finally Got a Gar)

MAY 17: Since I still hadn't caught a gar of my own, and since Hippy had caught one the day before, I vowed to return to the Chariton every day until I got one. Especially on the east side, where below the bridge to Youngstown, on the muddy edge of a long-gone railroad trestle twisted in a jagged tangle, where a rusty web of '40s cars was trussing back the bank, the big swilling cottonwood eddy was deep and dark and full of fish.

So I went there with my wife, Robin. But we didn't go to the steep side, because it had rained the night before and the slope was slick. Plus, we figured it would be easier to hang out on the sandy side.

Which we went down to even though it looked like rain. I had pretty much dragged her out to nature, and I could tell this wasn't what she had in mind. She wanted sun, but what we were getting were rumbly black thunderheads.

And whenever they rolled over, the fish splashed on the opposite side. The pressure was making them leap. And the more they leapt, the more I saw that a lot of them were gar, emerging white and tubular, then crescenting and splattering back. And the more I saw of that, the more the Gar Fever rose in me.

Then it started pouring.

"This sucks," Robin said, so we packed it up and went on home.

May 18: We returned with Hippy and a pair of hedge-clippers and I went chopping poison ivy down the trail. Because the steep side was still too

43

muddy and this place was now mine. Or, at least, I felt like claiming it and cutting back those evil leaves, because I was committed to getting a gar.

So we cast out our worms and sat there on the sand, fishing in the deepest hole for miles around. At most spots on the Chariton it's shallow enough to walk across—but only Jesus could do that here.

Then a front came rolling in and the fish started jumping again. The clouds, however, were not as dark as the day before and the threat of rain was minimal.

That's when I got a bite, set the hook, and reeled in some strange silver fish none of us had ever seen. It was a foot long and diamond-shaped with minnowy scales, shaddy fins, an upturned piranha-looking jaw, and a tongue covered in spiky fangs.

Which is the thing I love most about the River: You never know what you're going to catch.

Anyway, I let it go. It was bleeding from its mouth, though, and it instantly turned onto its side. So grabbing it, I pulled it backwards through the water, forcing water through its gills, giving it fish-CPR. It jumpstarted and swam away.

After that, we caught a gou (or drum, or sheepshead, or whatever they're called in your region), all purply-blue and hunchbacked with a pouty mouth. So I chopped it up and used it for bait.

It started clearing up and a bald eagle came flying downstream and passed right over us. We could see the yellow of its talons. Then ten minutes later, it came back from the other direction, clutching a chromy fish. No doubt, it was heading back to that giant aerie where Rye Creek meets the Chariton.

And that's all the day yielded: two measly fish and the glimmer of a patriotic raptor. And no gar whatsoever! Because when it comes to gar, I'm the biggest loser in town.

May 19: The Fever was up to 103 and the afternoon was sunny and clear, so I went by myself and scrambled down the concrete slabs on the steep side, side-stepping the poison ivy, until I got to the shore and set up two poles. One was my light-weight spinning rod with a worm on a panfish hook, and the other was a stiffer one with a big old Rhino-something-or-other closed-faced reel from Walmart equipped with sixty-five-pound test and a treble hook. That one got a night crawler, too.

On hot, bright days like this I'd normally be out on the lake, but now my allegiance was to the river, because it was packed full of gar. Which were tangible, so I figured, if I just hung out long enough.

And as the sun glared hotter and hotter, I sat on a rock, staring at the running boards and steering wheels poking up through the clay. It was a perfect place to catch some tetanus. Whoever decided to use these old cars to slow the erosion must've been an eco-genius. It had been decades since these junkers had been dumped down the bank, strung through with cable, then anchored to ancient pilings, but rust and rainbow chemicals were still mixing with the seepage coming through the mud.

Then doink! The tip of my wimpier rod signaled action, so I grabbed it and hauled back, reeling in another one of those oddball fish I'd caught the day before. This one, however, was smaller and less rhomboidal, more torpedo-shaped. And since I'd looked it up that morning, I knew what it was: a skipjack herring. But to me, it was bait.

"See ya later," I told that skipjack, cutting it in half. I put its head on my thicker pole, cast it upstream, re-wormed my lighter rod, and sat there for an hour or so, watching the minnows along the bank.

Till a long skinny form came nosing along, right on the surface. It was totally a gar! Two feet long and stalking prey! And it didn't see me right above it, reeling in and dangling my worm right beside it—which eventually spooked it, and it shot off.

As all this went on, I didn't even notice what was happening to the other rod. The thick green line was shooting out, then yanking my pole right off its stick. But I caught it, cranked back, and felt the hook sink into a heavy mass that immediately surfaced thirty feet away, thrashing like a mad bull.

It was a mongo lunker-gar, about five feet long and thicker than a big king salmon, all whitish gray with a big snapping gator-mouth gnashing at the line—probably upwards of thirty pounds!

Holy crap, was my first thought, *there's no way I can land this fish!*

In fact, I was afraid to even try—because I could see myself hauling it up onto the shore, but what would I do after that? I didn't have my net, so I'd have to tackle it. But with those razor-sharp incisors, it would surely rip me up. And since I'd read that a big gar's tail can bust a femur with a slap, my instinct was to just give up.

But I couldn't! Nope! This was the Big One, the Monster Gar of Missouri! Maybe it was even the New State Record. And there it was, just ten feet from shore.

I started reeling in and there was hardly any resistance at all, since its shape was conducive to getting hauled headfirst through the water. It was coming in easy. Too easy. But I kept the line tight. No Slack!

When I got it up beneath me, though, I knew there'd be trouble. Mainly, this fish was so jumbo that as soon as it saw me hovering above, it would shoot out and snap the line—as gar (I've read) are prone to do.

But it wasn't freaking out—which was weird. Maybe it'd been in similar situations before, so knew exactly what to do. Or maybe it didn't give a Wang Dang Doodle.

Still, I figured I should tire it out by letting it make another run. It was just too strong, too full of fury to pull in just like that. So I pressed the button and gave it some line and it rolled beneath me—big mistake! With that sudden slack, the barb popped out and it spit that chunk of skipjack out.

And as I looked down on it, shaking off the shock, I saw how truly massive it was. It was like a horse! I mean, I could've jumped down there and straddled it—because it was way huger than thirty pounds! Man, maybe it was even an alligator gar that'd been living in some farmer's pond for the past twenty years and had just been freed by the floods.

But like I said, it spit the hook out. And now it was starting to coil up beneath me like a rattlesnake about to spring. And as it gathered all that girth, it grew even huger. Until it sprang back into the current, leaving me agape in its wake.

It did rise, though, a minute later, twenty feet downriver. And as it did, it turned toward me and did that gesture with its chin, lifting it just a bit, as if to say, "What up, bro?"

Then it vanished, leaving me stewing in regret. Because I should of hauled it up on the bank, then sprang down there and pinned it to the mud! But I didn't. I let that chance go forever! What a stupid stupid Stupid!

But on the other hand, I was stoked immaculate because I had hooked a Mongo Gar! And other gar were definitely there and they were biting viciously!

So I tried to fish some more, but the climax was over and this was the dénouement—because God doesn't do encores.

May 20: The Fever was up to 104, the day wasn't too far behind, and since gar like it hot, I knew they'd be there again, patrolling their regular spots.

Gar are creatures of habit. If they stake out a hole, they'll probably be there the next day—so I was heading back.

This time I took Robin and my special gar rod rigged with hundred-pound super-test. She immediately caught a gou, which I immediately took a knife to and cut up for a sacrifice.

Then casting a drum-chunk out, we waited until a gar came along. It looked like the smaller one I had seen the day before, and by the way it was stalking minnows at the same time in the afternoon, I knew it was the exact same fish. We didn't try to catch it, though. We just let it swim on by.

In the meantime, the worms were roasting in the shade, it was 101 degrees, and I was dripping sweat and worried that Robin might've had enough. But sun was what she had come out for—not no stinking gar.

Then my other rod bowed and I set the hook. There was a big fish on the other end and the line instantly started zigging.

Yep, I thought, *I hooked that massive gar again!*

But when I brought it in closer, we saw it was just a river cat. And a big one at that—compared to the flatheads usually pulled from this hole. It was six pounds, all yellow-brown and calico.

I didn't give a hoot, though. Sure, I jumped down there and scooped it up and put it on a stringer—but so what? It was just an annoying beautiful fish getting in the way of gar.

Still, I cleaned it and fried it and the meat was sweet—but Big Whoopy Ding Dong! In short, the love was gone.

May 21: In the afternoon I went out alone, back to that same spot. It was cloudier and the gar were nowhere to be seen. But I did see a stripy brown water snake swimming downstream, and I did catch two gou—one of which I let go, but should've saved for bait. For some reason, though, I was feeling compassion for fish with pathetic expressions.

The way I looked at it now, my lighter-weight pole was for catching bait and my two stout poles were meant for the big ones. And if skipjack and drum died in the process, that wasn't much different than one hundred thousand-plus Iraqi civilians getting iced in the name of "Freedom."

Anyhow, my spinning rod started boinking, so I grabbed it. Because contrary to what I'd heard about letting gar run for twenty minutes, I'd been hooking gar (and so had Hippy) by just setting the hook good old-fashioned American-style.

So I set it and it caught. But what I reeled in was not a gar. It was a scrappy snapping turtle all covered with moss and medieval spikes, scrambling madly away from the bank. Then it bit the line, sending me home gar-less again, but determined to stick it out.

May 22: The fever was burning deliriously and since I was incapable of doing anything except trying to get a gar, I took Robin back to that spot and we went to the sandy side, where she could work on her tan.

It was sunny out and I caught a gou. Then chopped it up, baited up, and sat transfixed to both my lines. But no gar came along.

The eagle did, however, and there must've been a gyre up there, because it just kept circling us like the buzzards above the oblong pond on the other side of the road, where the Forest Lake Dam drains into a backwater full of bright yellow bullheads.

But other fish did not exist! Because only garfish mattered now! And it didn't matter if I drove myself nuts going to this spot and never getting jack! Since the river was thick with gar, I was playing the odds and couldn't stop. Yep, I was betting on gar and playing roulette for gar boulettes! And as soon as that ball landed on my number, I'd be digging up my recipe and whooping up a Cajun feast!

It had to happen soon. Statistics predicted it. So I kept on spinning that wheel . . .

May 23: I had to take a break—because if I went out there and got skunked again, I'd be totally bummed. So I went upstream to scope them out with Robin at Sandy Bottoms, where the road crosses the Chariton and a rogue canal cutting through the corn. It would be cool to paddle through the duckweed, I figured, and do some bobber fishing, too.

But there wasn't a spot on the shore not overgrown in poison ivy, so I said screw it. I wasn't going to take that chance.

We decided to head to Union Ridge instead, where there's a small crystal-clear lake filled with beaucoup water plants, where we'd always had luck with bass. But when we got out there, and after I'd caught three or four largemouth and didn't even laugh, I realized something had changed: me.

Aye, no longer did I care about the tangerine-bellied bluegills of my youth, which I used to be so mesmerized by. Or those splotchy old flathead cats with muscles busting from their backs. Or those spotted streamlined channel cats which had always seemed so feminine to me. No way! Who gives a crap about carp!? Or crappie!? Or even muskie!?

Not me, that's who! Because all the other fish in the world . . . they were just punks now! Because non-garfishing, that's kid stuff! Bass were so passé they'd become bassé. I didn't even care about bowfin or pike—for I had graduated to Gar!

Or so my line of thinking went. And I wondered what this meant for my Fish Future. Did it mean that I could never honestly take my nephew fishing? Would I be a liar sitting there with a worm on my line, not even giving a dang if some sunfish came along or not? Were all fish on the planet minus gar just some kind of pleasure-less food source?

And where was the loyalty? I mean, all my life I'd respected perch, smallmouth, blue cats, all the fish—and now I couldn't be bothered one lick. More than thirty years of catching fish, cleaning fish, reading, dreaming, researching fish, being genuinely in awe of fish! Yet here I was, willing to chuck them all, as if they never made me who I am.

Because I'm the Fish Guy: Billy Bass for Christmas! Fish shirts, fish ties, fish underwear, fish cetera! Fish on the Wall! Fish Fish Fish Fish Fish Fish Fish! Other Fish! Which, now, could just vanish forever—because gar were the Chosen Fish and I had a new identity, based on a fish I didn't know. Because gar were, and had always been, alien to me—so attractive because of mystery. Meaning, in essence, that I had no solid ground to stand on. Just a marshy bog of Lack!

All I knew was that I had to get back to the Chariton, which should be boring me by now, since every day it's the same old thing: drum after drum after drum after drum, while watching a watched pot! But the way I figured it, it was all a matter of putting in time.

So I came up with a new approach to keep me from becoming a junkie of that spot: From now on, I would go to that spot *every other day,* and explore new ones in between—in order to get a gar.

May 24: Hauling my gear down to the bank where I'd fought the Big One, I broke out my bag of frozen gou, cast out, and started waiting with no interest whatsoever in any fish that wasn't a gar—unless it could be used as bait.

Then IT hit again: the Humongous One I hooked the day before! It was the same color, the same size, in the same place at the same time, and under the same climactic conditions. And it was out there kicking up a fuss just like Jack Harper had described in that 1950 issue of *Outdoor Life*: "[T]hey call him gar. His mother is a hurricane and his father is a ring-tailed tornado, and when he's mad he's one fish wave of destruction."

Such a fish wave of destruction, in fact, that it started smacking around like an epileptic getting an exorcism, which proved to be an effective way of tossing off the hook. And then, just to tick me off, it waved goodbye with its tail.

Or maybe it was giving me the finger.

But at least I got to fight it again, the Mythic Lunker that always gets away. And I was glad for that, since that's way more than most people ever get. Because most people get dirt, then death, then dirt again. But I get fish on top of that. And hopefully . . . Gar.

May 25: We drove down south, scouting out places along the river, stopping on bridges and looking down. We were "gar-spotting," as Robin called it, because the Fever was up to 106.

Then half an hour out of town, we came to a bridge on a gravel road called Fountain Street, got out, and peered into the Chariton. And By Gar, it was filled with gar: black gar, gray gar, silver gar, white gar, yellow gar, Gar City USA! Some of them were two feet long, others three, and there were also fat old carp in there, as well as plenty of four-foot snakes winding all over the place and soft-shelled turtles too.

I didn't think it possible, but decided to give it a shot. There was a small gar right below me, about fifty feet beneath the bridge, swimming beside a logjam. And when I put my worm beside it, it immediately snapped sideways.

Now I'd been in this situation many times before and the hook had always popped out of its mouth. But since Hippy had caught a gar on a regular hook on regular line, I figured I could do the same, despite all the authorities who say to let gar hork down the bait, even if it takes half an hour. So I set that hook as if it were a catfish, and it caught, and we fought, and it twisted off in less than a minute.

Goll-Dangit! I decided to give it a few more tries. But each time I set the hook, the same thing happened. Until eventually we ran out of worms.

I'd brought along some frozen gou, though, so I cut off a chunk of tail, picked out a yellowy gar, and dropped it right beside its head.

And slowly, languidly, it twisted sideways and picked it off the bottom. I decided to give it some time to swallow and it took off downstream and I gave it more line. And more and more and more and more line. I let it run for a few more minutes, and then I couldn't take it anymore, so hauled back and set that hook.

WHANG! The gar leapt, slapping and flapping sixty yards downstream. It was only a three-pounder, but I got it back to the bridge, and then it was in the air and coming up and my cheapo reel couldn't even handle it. I had to set the drag tighter while it spiraled beneath me, suspended above the river.

Then horsing and horsing and horsing it in, I started fearing I would lose it. All it had to do was snap at the right angle and it'd shake itself off like all those other gar I lost.

So I torqued back and sent that fish flying up and it landed on the concrete beside me, all twenty-five inches of it! Which I grabbed! Finally I had a gar! Sleek and phallic with needly teeth!

WOW!! We were cheering and clapping and jumping up and down. Because I was no longer a gar virgin! It had happened! So now I could go swaggering around like a Total Gar Stud!

But did I throw it back? Nope, not this one! Since there were tons down there and none in our fridge, I stuck my knife through its head, took it home, cut it open (weird clay-blue eggs!), then fleshed it out and began my guerilla taxidermy.

I use a method from the '50s, which relies on Borax, a product that doesn't exist anymore, except as a "laundry booster." Still, that stuff had worked on two muskellunge—one which I mounted on an old tire, the other on a couple of cow pies. What I do is coat the skin with Borax inside, sew the belly back together, funnel it full of sand, and let it dry in the sun. After a few weeks, I pour the sand out and pump the shell full of insulating foam. With this fish, though, I decided to fill it with Ping Pong balls, then construct a gut out of Bondo later, which would make it look fatter.

As for the tube of meat, I skinned it out, flayed off the backbone, cut out all the ribs, and took what was left of it (11.5 ounces) and ground that up in a food processor with half an onion, half a cup of bread crumbs, a jalapeno pepper, half a cup of parsley and green onions from the garden, a dash of salt and pepper, and a beaten egg. Then I made twelve golf ball-sized boulettes, rolled them in flour, browned them in cooking oil, threw in the other half of the onion (chopped), added a cup of water, a half-cup of white wine, then simmered it all for forty-five minutes and served it over rice with the sauce from the pan.

Robin thought my balls tasted great. She said they had a complex taste.

May 27: The most important thing about getting that gar was that I finally got over not getting a gar. That is, now that I had bagged a two-foot short-nose, I didn't feel compelled to go to the Chariton every day because I lacked a fish on my list.

So last night at dusk, I went back to the lily pads, found myself a tight-lining spot, cast a chicken liver out, kicked back, and waited as the bullfrogs blurped.

Eventually, a cat came along, chomped on, and I was psyched to reel it in: a sassy, sexy four-pound beauty, all golden and perfect and rattling in that channel-cat way. She was so hot I had to kiss her. Then I let her go.

Meanwhile, it's good to know there's still a Mammoth Gar out there circling that big ol' hole and taunting me to take another shot. Which is what drives me now—to see it again, meet it again, then battle it again—not really caring if I catch it or not. Because maybe it can't be caught. And if that's the case, so much the better—to have an elusive creature out there amidst the tires and axles and mufflers corroding in the Chariton.

But if I get it, I'm not so sure I'll restrain myself from whooping up two hundred gar balls. Next time, though, I think I'll use some garlic in the mix.

Afterword

I keep pondering that Mongo Gar, wondering what kind it was. It was the size of a longnose, but longnose only eat live fish and its bill didn't strike me as skinny enough. It was way too big to have been a shortnose or spotted, and since it's highly unlikely that an alligator gar could exist so far north, it might've been a hybrid—between a longnose and a shortnose or a spotted.

Such crossbreeds are extremely rare in the wild, but the Upper Midwest Environmental Sciences Center does list spotted/longnose hybrids on their species list, and longnose/shortnose hybrids have been reported in Wisconsin.

6

When Gars Attack

IT'S CURIOUS THAT the January 22, 1922, garticle "Alligator Gar More Dangeroous [*sic*] Than So-Called 'Man Eater' Shark," does not have a writer attached to it, but it would be pushing it to suggest that this is because the author was trying to protect himself from publicizing folly. Like most of the articles in the New Orleans's *Times-Picayune* at that time, there were no bylines; meaning it was probably written by a staff writer.

But whatever the case may be, this article did little to advance anyone's knowledge of gar. In fact, it did the exact opposite by sensationalizing the entire species through subheads reading "Many Authentic Instances of Human Beings Being Attacked Especially While Standing in Water" and "Only One Case of Man Being Attacked by Shark." The result was a plethora of piscine plume-pushers referencing this work of "journalism" for more than eighty-five years.

Whereas some fish writers have been skeptical of this article, the brunt of ichthyologic ink leans toward a certain historical respect for what it has to say. Which, in part, is this: "There is an instance recorded of the killing of a human being by a 'man-eater' shark something over ninety years ago, but unfortunately it is not possible to say whether this occurrence was thoroughly investigated or not."

Of course, it is also not possible to say whether the information in this anonymous article was "thoroughly investigated or not," but that doesn't matter to our unknown author, who went on to stress that there is no evidence of an alligator, crocodile, or bear ever attacking a human, but (and this is basically his implication) there are roving gangs of alligator gar out there eager to bust down your door and go postal on your family!

That's my own embellishment of how the article operates, because that's what it tries to do: paint gator gar as more ferocious than other creatures known for ripping into humans. And it does a pretty good job of that.

This article, however, is full of typos and other mistakes that do not bolster its authority, and destabilize its credibility. For instance, our enigmatic author states that there are three types of gar in Louisiana, when even back then it was common knowledge that there were four kinds in the state. Also, it says that the Louisiana Department of Conservation knows the habits of gar "fairly well"—a statement it later contradicts in the section titled "LITTLE KNOWN OF 'GATOR GAR.'" Then we're offered this little gem, with no segue whatsoever: "If you should happen to emerge from a bath in one of the bays or streams on the coast of the Gulf of Mexico next summer with an arm or a leg missing or so badly mangled that you have no further use for it, do not bring the customary indictment against the shark or the alligator, both of whom can prove a satisfactory "alibi," but present the alligator gar to the grand jury, and you will have little trouble in obtaining the return of a true bill or in convicting him on expert testimony."

Fear tactics are then employed in lines like "There are instances too numerous to be recounted to show that he will attack human beings" and "EVERY ONE KILLED IS HELP."

But where's the proof? This isn't journalism. This is anti-gar propaganda!

Nevertheless, a case is made regarding gar attacks on human beings, with the first charge coming from "David Starr Jordan, an authority of worldwide fame," who mentioned a gar killing an Italian barber bathing "off Spanish Fort a few years ago." This is no doubt the incident referred to by Edward Ricciuti in *Killers of the Seas,* who made the mistake of claiming that these details came from a letter.

This suspect second-hand info (which is probably actually third- or fourth-hand), is supported by hearsay from an unnamed "conservation official," who was "one of the most experienced hunters and fishermen in the state." The story of Maj. William Arms, a "crack rifle shot of the Washington Artillery," is then relayed. Seems he was cleaning squirrels on Bayou La Branche when he "unconsciously dropped his hand in the water," attracting a gar "about nine feet long." Allegedly, it chomped on and dragged the major into the water. His pal, however, sprang into action with an axe, and the major's hand was extracted from the fish.

Such stories, involving hands and feet getting munched on by gar, are not uncommon—as our ambiguous author demonstrates by once again citing the official, who enters into evidence the experience of a certain Mrs. Taige. While washing laundry in Bayou des Allemandes, she was supposedly seized by some sort of pet gar, which fishermen at Camp Coco Taige had been feeding for years.

This indictment is followed by an often-referred-to-but-still-unverified account of how an employee of the State Museum was fishing with a friend and his son "in Little Lake, in the Barataria section." According to legend, there were gar feeding on refuse (in some accounts it's "offal") being thrown from the boat, when the kid decided to plop his little piggies in. Reportedly, a big old gar clamped on and a struggle ensued. The child was almost pulled from the boat, but the men used oars to bonk the gar, until finally it released the boy, who was probably nicknamed Stumpy after that.

Thus, we have another fish tale in the tradition of C. C. Abbott's "An Ugly Customer," published in an 1867 edition of *Riverside Magazine.* Abbot claims to have witnessed an angler plunge "his arm in the water to seize a shad that was about to escape, and before he had reached the escaping shad, the gar made a dash at him, seizing him just above the hand, and held on so tenaciously that the man bitten dragged the gar into the batteau, and then was compelled to cut the jaws of the animal before he could free himself."

Abbott's story, however, did not register in the public consciousness to the degree that the *Times-Picayune* article did. Whereas Abbot's article was essentially entertainment reading (it preceded a story titled "Uncle Ainslee's Squirrel Story" and was lumped among works of fiction), the anonymous article was published in a type of media expected to be factual.

The 1922 article also mentioned physician James Giggett, who then takes the virtual stand in the case of Alligator Gar vs. the People of the United States. Supposedly, back when Dr. Gigget was a college student, he was wading in a spot in the Mississippi where three other students had recently been killed by what were reported to be sharks, when he was "seized by a fish, and he was drawn under." According to our ambiguous journalist, Gigget escaped, but not without injury: "The marks on the foot of young Gigget . . . showed he was attacked by an alligator gar, and the conclusion as to the other three was revised accordingly."

We are told that this "matter is of record in the State University at Baton Rouge." Still, there is no reference whatsoever to the specific location of this information at Louisiana State University. It therefore appears that our alligator gar know-it-all merely repeated some sketchy stories and passed them off as fact.

Anyway, despite the obvious holes in this article, it was seminal in establishing the gar's reputation as a blood-thirsty, man-eating monster lurking in both fresh and salt water—which, in a way, made it okay for other judges to condemn Cajun barracudii based solely on witness testimony, rather than solid evidence.

But there are other factors to take into account, like statistics, when it comes to sharks. As David Johnson asserts in his article "Sharks! Myths and Statistics about the Oceans' Most Fearsome Creature," the number of actual shark "attacks is hard to determine because of poor reporting in many areas." Plus, "News about shark attacks is often repressed so tourists will not be driven away."

Poor reporting aside, it's also important to consider that we are now in an era that pays more attention to data than back in the '20s. For instance, there were plenty of alligator gar caught in Missouri in the nineteenth and twentieth centuries which weighed well over 200 pounds, but none were acknowledged by the state until 2001, when an extremely rare 115-pounder was killed by a bowhunter near Cape Girardeau.

And it's pretty much the same for other states, which kept track of other lunkers for decades, but refused to recognize gator gar as a fish worthy of attention. Unless, that is, some dummy cleaning fish happened to drop his hand in the water during a feeding frenzy.

But as Johnson notes, "between 1580 and 2004 there were 1,969 confirmed shark attacks around the world," with the brunt of them (761) being in American waters. So with a bit of extrapolation, here's where the score stands today:

Confirmed shark attacks = 2000
Confirmed gar attacks = 0

These figures, however, aren't too surprising, considering that there have always been reports of alien abductions, Sasquatch sightings, Loch Ness monsters, ghosts, goblins, flying saucers, angels, et cetera. Accounts which, I hereby verify, are way more common than valid reports of Gars Gone Wild.

As noted by the Missouri Sportsmen's Information Network, "Despite their intimidating size and teeth . . . alligator gar are not aggressive and pose no threat to Missouri fishermen." A statement backed up by the Florida Museum of Natural History, whose online info on the *Lepisosteiformes* affirms that "there is no documentation of attacks on man by alligator gar."

Ultimately, though, those who are closest to gar know that they've been swimming with people for centuries—no problem! A point made by trophy fisherman Steve Ryan in his article "Leave the Bacon in the Fridge," when he recounts how he "hopped into the water with a 7-foot-plus, 150-pound alligator gar" to swim with it while he released it.

Captain Kirk, foreground, and Dave Rothstein pose with a smiling gar on the Trinity River in Texas. Photo courtesy of Steve Ryan.

If you take a look at this fish, you'll see the truth for yourself. Like many alligator gars caught on film, this fish's expression is way more comic than vicious, due to the naturally happy camber of its upturned crocodile smile.

So if you should take a swim this summer and emerge from a river missing a leg, don't go and blame the alligator gar, but look to piranhas instead. Or Al Qaeda, or domestic abuse, or E.coli, or nicotine, or our fear of the unknown—which all have verified histories of crippling and killing humans. Because when it comes to gar, all we have are fish stories.

7

Some Messy Nessie Gar Myths
& Other Distortions

AFTER MONTHS AND MONTHS of reading about sea monsters in American waters, I came up with a theory that wherever such creatures are reported, there's a history of two things: 1) imaginations that are aware of previous regional stories, because certain details keep getting repeated, and 2) big fish. So I started looking into it.

It seemed logical to start with Lake Champlain, a 109-mile-long body of water located between New York and Vermont and reaching into Quebec. There's a legend there of a plesiosaurus-type Loch Ness monster lurking beneath the surface. The primary sighting was credited to the French explorer Samuel de Champlain, the first European discoverer of the lake. In 1609, he allegedly saw a "20-foot serpent thick as a barrel and [with] a head like a horse." Since then, there have been over three hundred sightings of "Champ," and subsequently, a tourist industry thriving off T-shirts, bumper stickers, Champ-burgers, and visitors with binoculars searching for North America's most celebrated monster next to Bigfoot.

The thing is, Champlain never claimed to see any sort of sea serpent. What he did claim to see was a fish known to the Iroquois Indians as "Chaousarou." According to his journals, translated in *The Works of Samuel de Champlain, vol. II,* Champlain saw:

> some five feet long, which were as big as my thigh, and had a head as large as my two fists, with a snout two feet and a half long, and a double row of very sharp, dangerous teeth. Its body has a good deal the shape of the pike; but it is protected by scales of a silvery gray colour and so strong that a dagger could not pierce them. The end of its snout is like a pig's. This fish makes war on all the other fish which are in these lakes and rivers. And, according to what these tribes have told me, it shows marvellous ingenuity in that,

when it wishes to catch birds, it goes in amongst the rushes or reeds which lie along the shores of the lake in several places, and puts its snout out of the water without moving. The result is that when the birds come and light on its snout, mistaking it for a stump of wood, the fish is so cunning that, shutting its half-open mouth, it pulls them by their feet under the water.

Champlain's illustration of this fish can be found on his map of 1612; it is clearly labeled "Chaousarou" and it is clearly a gar. Still, there was no stopping the machinery of distortion that occurred during the following two centuries.

According to Joe Nickell's "Legend of the Lake Champlain Monster," published in *The Skeptical Inquirer*, back in 1819, a certain Captain Crum on a scow in Bulwagga Bay reported a black monster "said to be about 187 feet long with its flat head—resembling that of a 'sea-horse'—rearing more than fifteen feet out of the water. The creature was some two hundred yards away (twice the length of a football field) and was traveling 'with the utmost velocity' while being chased by 'two large Sturgeon and a Bill-fish.'" Nevertheless, from 600 feet away the captain was able to notice that it had three teeth, large eyes the color of "a pealed [*sic*] onion," a white star on its forehead, and "a belt of red around the neck."

This story, of course, was repeated for generations as fishermen and hunters flocked to Lake Champlain to catch the source of so many wild stories. Then, in 1880, P. T. Barnum fed the frenzy further by offering a $50,000 reward for Champ, dead or alive.

Numerous sightings followed, with the majority of them indicating a multiple-humped leviaform ranging from twenty to fifty feet in length. Some descriptions, however, claimed the body structure to be alligator-

Samuel de Champlain's gar illustration, 1612. Photo courtesy of Beinecke Rare Book and Manuscript Library.

like, whereas others declared it to be more serpentine. Many reported it splashing around in the mud (like gar do when they're spawning), whereas others focused on its tendency to rise for air. These details and others contributed to the inspiration for the Hollywood movie *Lake Placid*, in which a mongo mutant alligator terrorizes vacationers.

Still, a good percentage of the sightings stray from the super-spectacular, indicating a creature four to ten feet long, often described as gray in color and "log-" or "pole-like"—which isn't too surprising, considering that longnose gar and sturgeon are both indigenous to the area and sometimes caught by fishermen.

As for evidence of such a behemoth actually existing, there isn't much beyond Sandra Mansi's highly contested 1977 photograph of a Loch Ness Monster look-alike, and the testimony of some individuals—many repeat offenders, party boat revelers, and plenty of them anonymous.

Anyhow, the Vermont House of Representatives eventually took notice of the hype and passed a law protecting "North America's Loch Ness Monster" from "any willful act resulting in death, injury, or harassment." The New York State Senate and Assembly followed suit, adding to the intrigue of a gar description blown out of proportion.

There's a similar case in Arkansas, where the state legislature created the White River Monster Refuge and passed a law making it illegal for anybody to harm, bother, or hunt the legend known as Whitey. Whereas experts have speculated that what witnesses observed was a trapped elephant seal that had worked its way up from the Gulf of Mexico, it's relevant to note that early reports of this creature state it to be long and gray, about twelve feet in length, partial to floating on the surface, and resembling a sturgeon or catfish. The word "gar," however, is hardly ever associated with the White River Monster—which is suspicious, considering that this region was once world famous for its colossal alligator gars.

Lake Conway, Arkansas, where I now live, also has a history of a fabled monster. The Lake Conway Monster has been reported to be everything from a "skunk ape" to an octopus. As Joe Mosby reports in the December 6, 2003, edition of *Arkansas News:* "In the early 1950s, numerous reports were made about a strange and unidentified creature seen, heard and—on one or two alleged occasions—smelled in and around the lake. Guesses included bear, escaped convict, alligator, alligator snapping turtle and—most frequently and most likely—alligator gar."

Another southern lake-monster swimming with the gars is the Altamaha-Ha, near Darien, Georgia, with a cousin in Jacksonville, Florida. The first sighting of this snakelike enigma dates back to 1969, when Donny

Manning saw a ten- to twelve-foot unidentified swimming object with what looked like a cross between an alligator and a platypus snout. This creature was "gun-metal gray on top and oyster white-yellow on the bottom." It reportedly breached like a dolphin, and was estimated to be upwards of seventy-five pounds.

By 1980, though, the Altamaha-Ha was reported to be thirty to forty feet long, and "as big around as a man's body" (a recurring characteristic, indicating that enthusiastic witnesses were familiar with the details of previous sightings). Other repeating themes were the alligator snout, its prehistoric look, its log-like shape, its grayish coloring, its penchant for floating on the surface, and its resemblance to sturgeon. Still, alligator gar are always left out of the comparisons (as if this might give it away), even though numerous reports indicate it to be ten to twelve feet long.

Then there's the Lake Murray Monster in South Carolina, known as Messie, described by *The Independent News* in 1980 as "a cross between a snake and something prehistoric." This legendary big one has supposedly torn up fishing nets (a behavior alligator gar are known for) and has a history of anonymous callers to radio stations charging that there's a monster out there. Messie has also been accused of being a sturgeon, but, curiously, the possibility of it being a garfish is never mentioned in the reports.

There has been speculation, however, that the Lake Norman Monster in Mooresville, North Carolina, could be a gar. Or, for that matter, a sturgeon, alligator, catfish, eel, snakehead, etc.

A giant serpent-creature named One Eye in Lake Granby, Texas, also has a body of lore, this one dating back to "ancient Native Americans" who sacrificed animals to it. Spanish settlers in the area allegedly observed this creature, but, like the countless monsters across the continent that people swear they see but fail to catch (on camera or in the flesh), old One Eye is still awaiting verification.

The point being: All across America—but especially in the South, where gar are most plentiful—there are reports of long, serpentine, land-locked leviathans that grow larger and larger through the decades. And in most cases, the brunt of available information on these "monsters" is posted on Chamber of Commerce websites.

One explanation for the popularity of these accounts has to do with excitement generated by European newspapers reporting on eyewitness accounts during the settling of the country. According to Craig Ogilve's article "Legendary Arkansas Monsters Have Deep Roots in History," "The fact that Arkansas was sparsely settled in the early nineteenth century helped create many of the original legends. Isolated and with virtually no social activities, families entertained themselves with folktales they had heard or ones they fabricated on the spot."

Lee Krystek's article "The Misplaced Monster of the White River," however, offers this explanation for Whitey: "Biologist and cryptozoologist Roy P. Mackal looked at the evidence and decided 'the White River case is a clear-cut instance of a known aquatic animal outside its normal habitat or range and therefore . . . [it is often misidentified by] observers unfamiliar with the type.'"

Michael Meurger and Claude Gagnon, in discussing author Brian Vachon's flawed journalism on Champ, offer another explanation in their book *Lake Monster Traditions: A Cross-Cultural Analysis* (1988):

> Brian Vachon is typical of many modern writers who have perpetuated a falsehood through laziness. In his article about the Lake Champlain monster he writes: "The oldest hint about the existence of a strange animal has been given by the very man who gave his name to the lake." He [Vachon] actually uses parts of Champlain's account, yet the name "Chaousarou" does not appear, giving the impression of an unknown animal. And what is worse is that he has taken the fragment of Champlain's account and presented it as part of a secular tradition, when he writes: "According to the stories that have been told for generations . . ." Such inaccuracies, enthusiastically copied and transmitted by journalists, eventually become "established fact."

Similarly, a study cited in *Discover* magazine's April 1998 feature on the Lake Champlain Monster indicates that pandas reported missing from a zoo in the Netherlands led to a "psychological contagion" responsible for hysteria. The conclusion being: "People tend to see pandas and monsters . . . if told to look for them." Likewise, Nickell refers to the idea of "expectant attention" and suggests that it plays a part in people believing they saw a monster.

Ultimately, though, the seiche theory, discussed in the same issue of *Discover*, offers the most plausible explanation of plesiosaur sightings. Since Lake Champlain and Loch Ness share similar topographies, there's a phenomenon that occurs in both bodies of water during the summer, a.k.a. tourist season, when most Champ/Nessie sightings take place. The seiche effect is described as similar to a body rising from a bathtub, which causes water to rush in and fill the vacated space, thereby resulting in a wave sploshing back and forth across the surface until it peters out. When this happens in long, deep lakes like Loch Ness and Lake Champlain, submerged matter can be churned up and carried for days, often trailing a wake.

The key to the mystery of North America's Loch Ness Monster, however, is in Champlain's original description of chaousarou. Champlain notes that this fish has "a double row of very sharp, dangerous teeth," yet longnose gar only have a single row of teeth. Since the only member of the species that has two rows of teeth (on the upper jaw) is the alligator gar, we can deduce that what Champlain actually saw was an old school gator gar harking back to the days when they used to range as far north as Canada. This possibility, of course, is about as likely as an elephant seal swimming hundreds of miles upstream, but these things do happen. And when they do, the previously mentioned factors of "psychological contagion" and "expectant attention" are more likely to occur.

Meaning it's not too unusual for an out-of-context alligator gar to get larger and stranger every time it's mused upon. Hence, it's not unreasonable to consider that when people see big gar, something in the story-making mechanism of the imagination gets stimulated. Consciously or not, this frequently results in making stuff up. Phenomena like the seiche effect, deceptive scholarship, and boredom due to isolation then get added to the equation, confusing matters even more. Consequently, we end up paying more attention to the prospect of *the supernatural* rather than *the natural*—which can be just as fantastic, if not more.

But whatever the explanation is, as Nickell notes, "One cannot draw a conclusion from a lack of knowledge, and so, until an actual specimen presents itself, the possibility that any large, unknown animal inhabits Lake Champlain remains somewhere between extraordinarily slim and none."

Meanwhile, we now have tons of stories about weird, unidentified creatures swimming in our midst. In some cases they are viewed as myths, and in others they are marketed as tourist attractions. But in all instances, no conclusive evidence has been offered yet that can prove that monsters really exist.

8

Mutant Gar Is Missing Link

I N MAY OF 2006 the JPEGs began pouring in. Since family and friends knew that I had a bad case of Gar Fever, and since it was obvious that the recently discovered fossil remains of *Tiktaalik roseae* in the Arctic looked like a freaky gar, the newspaper clippings soon followed. And as all this information came in, I did some research of my own, and even contacted Dr. Neil H. Shubin of the University of Chicago Department of Organismal Biology and Anatomy, who was in on the discovery.

The result is the following proclamation:

Hear Ye, Hear Ye! I Hereby Officially Establish That The Existence Of *Tiktaalik* Proves That Humans Evolved From Gar!

As Darwin predicted in his P.S. to C. Lyell in his letter of 1860, "*Our ancestor was an animal which breathed water, had a swim bladder, a great swimming tail, [and] an imperfect skull.*"

The proof is in the scree. Right at the top of North America, in the Nunavut region of Canada (which used to be part of Euramerica back in the Devonian days), there were four- to-nine-foot crocodile-headed fish with wrist-like bones in their front fins for crawling out of the muck. Because 375 million years ago, this area had a subtropical, fluvial geography, much like that of the Mississippi Delta today—which, of course, is an ideal habitat for gar.

Not only that, but *Tiktaalik* (which is Inuit for *big fish living in the shallows*) shares other characteristics with its gar-descendants from the Cretaceous. Both gar and *Tiktaalik* have diamond-shaped scale patterns common to the *Crossopterygii* class (represented by coelacanths and rhipidistians), from which lungfish, bowfin and gar evolved. According to Edward Daeschler et al. (who announced their findings in the April 6, 2006, issue of *Nature*), "The dorsal surface of *Tiktaalik* is covered with rhombic, overlapping, tuberculated scales." And according to Dr. Shubin,

Tiktaalik's scales are similar to those of the *Lepisosteids* (the gar family)—which, in Greek, means *bony scales.*

Dr. Shubin informs me that *Tiktaalik*'s teeth are "a combination of fangs and denticles; fangs on the coronoids, vomer, etc., and denticles on the dentary." These predator teeth are structured in two rows (similar to the alligator gar), and are handy for chomping down on all sorts of swampy prey—just like gar.

Dr. Shubin also notes that *Tiktaalik* has nostrils, "both internal and external"—just like gar.

As for *Tiktaalik*'s "imperfect skull," Daeschler uses the term "elpistostegalian" to indicate its paraphyletic grade of flat-headedness among the "finned sarcopterygians that lie along the tetrapod stem lineage." *Tiktaalik*'s body, however, is tubular and streamlined—just like gar.

Plus, both species "lack the anterior dorsal fins and possess broad, dorsoventrally compressed skulls with dorsally placed eyes, paired frontal bones, marginal nares and a subterminal mouth"—just like gar.

Tiktaalik's curving ribcage indicates that it had the same type of lung-like organs that gar have, which are convenient when it comes to "specializations for spiracular breathing across the aquatic-terrestrial interface"—an accessory that made it possible for *Tiktaalik* to pull itself up on the

Tiktaalik Roseae, Arctic. Photo by Beth Rooney for the University of Chicago.

mud front-wheel-drive style and breathe oxygen for a spell. The refrain continues.

But the most complicated feature of this *fishapod* (a creature filling the gap between tetrapod and fish), which makes it the morphological bridge between *Panderichthys* (the fish it once was) and *Acanthostega* (the gator-like creature it became), are the endochondral bones in the pectoral fins which suggest a fingerlike functionality found in primates. And this, of course, is wigging out the fundamentalists.

A month after the announcement of the breakthrough discovery of *Tiktaalik,* the Internet is buzzing with controversy. Whereas scientists are saying that *Tiktaalik* is just one of many intermediates between species, the non-believers are basically saying that *Tiktaalik* does not fill a gap, because it creates two more. But as John Noble Wilford states in *The New York Times* article "Fossil Called Missing Link from Sea to Land Animals," these fossils are "a powerful rebuttal to religious creationists, who have long argued that the absence of such transitional creatures are a serious weakness in Darwin's theory." And as Dr. Michael J. Novacek, a paleontologist for the American Geographic Society, adds, "We've got Archaeopteryx, an early whale that lived on land, and now this animal showing the transition from fish to tetrapod. What more do we need from the fossil record to show that the creationists are flatly wrong?"

Denial of scientific fact, however, is an inherent feature of "intelligent design," whose proponents have tried to manipulate science into showing that dinosaurs and cavemen existed at the same time, a few thousand years before Christ.

Take Carl Baugh, for example, who championed the now-debunked Texas "man-track" claim made in 1987, when he found a fossilized tooth near some dinosaur prints southwest of Fort Worth. As Ronnie J. Hastings remarks in "A Tale of Two Teeth," "this tooth was hailed as contributing to the death knell of evolutionary theory. It allegedly proved that dinosaurs and humans lived simultaneously in a world whose history is better explained by Genesis than modern science."

Still, Baugh's research quickly undid any credibility he might have had. For one thing, he used the observations of dentists to confirm that this tooth was human. But when "Little David" (as he called it) was sent to labs at Texas Christian University and the University of Texas, the results came back that the tooth was "similar to specimens . . . on hand" and was identified as "an incisiform tooth from an extinct primitive bony fish called [a pycnodont] . . . ancestral to the gar."

Meanwhile, more and more analysis took place of similar teeth found at the site where Little David was discovered. The upshot being that Baugh, having denied the findings of his colleagues, eventually got, according to Hastings, "the tooth, the whole tooth, and nothing but the tooth."

Thus, scientific observation logically concludes that it is no longer a leap in faith to claim that the earliest type of alligator on this planet came from the earliest type of gar.

The irony in all of this is that it took 375 million years for garosaurs to evolve into humans (who use empirical evidence to trace the path of what they evolved from), but there are still those among us who would rather we dismiss what we've learned about traits that connect us to "lower life-forms." Because what if we didn't just come from apes . . . what if we came from fish as well? And not just any fish, but the lowliest of the lowliest? The ones we slaughter and scatter on the shore! The ones we love to hate!

So chalk another one up for gar, for continuing to scare the pants off those who fear what we might discover about the special selection of ourselves if we really listened to ourselves—which could lead us to confess that we are not the selves we believe ourselves to be as indicated in certain texts that teach us moral lessons, but don't quite tell us how to deal with the revelation that we come from the most demonstrative fish on earth.

Meaning a whole new can of worms has been opened—and it's full of living, breathing, land-roving gar. So forget about monkeys, *Homo sapiens!* The missing link has been discovered, and gar are our forefathers.

9

How I Finally Bagged the Big One

TEXAHOMA WAS TOTALLY FLOODED, from Tulsa to Houston and beyond, but Captain Kirk said, "Come on down! It's been raining all week, the river's thirty feet over its crest, but the ladies are biting. Today we got a 165-pounder, and yesterday we caught nine over a hundred." So Hippy and I were bombing down to Huntsville.

I was expecting controversy. Scott Perry, who directed the 1997 Troma film *Teenage Catgirls in Heat*, had e-mailed me about some guides who were taking trophy bowhunters into the spawning grounds of the last endangered Texas alligator gars. These clowns would start the day with a prayer to the Lord, asking for luck in smearing big gar that could very well be a century old, then they'd go in there and shoot 'em up. They were taking two-hundred-pounders and there was nothing anyone could do, because in Texas, gator gar aren't considered game fish.

But when Captain Kirk pulled up to the Motel 6 at 5:00 a.m., and when we were in his truck and rolling past the misty prisons in the still-dark night, he waved my fears away.

"The spawn is up!" he told us. "Like back in '83 and '93! It's the best I've seen in over a decade. Those stupids can't do anything!"

And as dusk came up, we found ourselves on the Trinity River, the gar boat gliding over the murky water, which was running hard and full of foam, logs, plastic bottles, and exploded coolers from years ago, lost in creeks and freed by the floods. It was the same stretch Hippy and I had fished by ourselves after getting skunked a year ago with the captain, who had granted us a free day, so we had gone and bought another.

By the time the sun rose, Kirk was breaking out the bait and we were setting up the rod holders along the muddy bank. They were spaced about forty yards apart, and all of them were equipped with alarms. We had five heavy-duty Shakespeare PowerRods equipped with hundred-pound woven test, and if the line should start going out on any of them, a high-pitched squealing sound would be emitted and we'd zoom back from the other side where we'd be anchored and waiting for gar.

Over the next few hours it happened a couple of times, but each time we went on over and grabbed the rod, the gar would drop the bait, then vanish like the rain—which had come down the night before. But for some strange reason, the rain was leaving us alone that morning while pouring down on the rest of the state.

"The gar-gods must be smiling on us," I told Hippy.

But not that much, because out there in the overcast, we spent the next few hours watching soccer balls go floating by. And basketballs and Nerf balls and baseballs and random tires and thousands of stumps and even a bobbing mannequin. Till eventually it was almost eleven and I was starting to wonder if I'd ever get a monster seven-footer like the one that had triggered my Gar Fever as a kid.

"Shucks," I said, "let's make some sandwiches."

Which was pretty much the equivalent of saying, "Okay Hippy, let's give it up," because the gar weren't even porpoising.

But as soon as we laid out the seedy bread, cheddar cheese, mayo, mustard, and chicken meat, one of the alarms went off.

"Let's Roll!" Captain Kirk gave the command.

I stuffed the stuff back in my bag, Hippy undid the bowline, and we shot across the torrent of diapers and plastic bags and unidentified floating objects swilling down from Dallas-Fort Worth.

When we hit the shore, I grabbed the rod and Captain Kirk threw it in reverse. In less than a minute, we were floating after and the line was going out and going fast. So I kept feeding more and more into the river, thinking that this gar will drop it, like they always do.

"Come on, girl," Captain Kirk called to the gar, then told me to start reeling in the slack.

That's when we hit the river bend where the banks were high and chunks of land kept falling in because the soil was loaded with water weight. There was a big old eddy there swilling full of yellow froth, Mountain Dew cans, bleach jugs, oil containers, Styrofoam, two-by-fours, and even a bloated cow reeking with flies.

"Where's the float?" Captain Kirk asked. "Where'd it go?"

I thought it was strange that he would ask, but I thought it even stranger that we were still chasing the gar. We'd been after it for fifteen minutes, but maybe it was off the line.

"Okay," Captain Kirk said, "start reeling in, and when you feel her, set the hook."

I started reeling in a football field's worth of line while we whorled around in the whirling swirl. And as the line began getting tighter, we could see the path of the fish below. It was right beneath us, deep deep down, moving clockwise, and the float was nowhere to be seen.

Suddenly the line went taut, so I lowered the rod, then hauled back, jerking it as hard as I could. And somewhere leagues beneath us, I felt my distant hook sink into a mass of meat.

"Set It Again!" Captain Kirk shouted, so I set it again. Then he yelled it four more times, so I set the hook four more times. And each time I did it, it made a run, spinning the drag on that oversized reel.

"She's a big one!" Captain Kirk said.

For every twenty yards I'd reel in, it took another thirty out. But what was I going to do? Lay down my pole and give up? No Way! I kept on raising that rod, then reeling in as I lowered it, while two old boys in a flat-bottomed boat fished for catfish on the far bank.

After twenty-five minutes, I finally got it under the boat, and then it passed right under us—and kept passing under us. Even Captain Kirk whistled in awe. That thing was at least six feet long and as thick around as a kayak, with scales the size of dominoes. Then I saw an eyeball turn. It saw us, went wide, and that gar shot off like a shoplifter, taking out another thirty yards.

I hauled back and hauled back while Hippy and Kirk kept yelling stuff. My back was starting to ache, my arms were getting tired, and I didn't think it possible. Because this was the mythical Big One—so there was no way I could ever get it in the boat. It was destined to bust the line, bend the hook, and take off like the rest, leaving me someone who always gets close but no cigar.

Then I got it alongside again.

"Ya Stupid!" Captain Kirk said to the gar. "You're hooked by a hair!"

The treble was lodged in one of the gills, one tiny barb connecting two creatures—one just under two hundred pounds, and the other at least half of that. Then the gar shot off again.

But I yanked it in and it saw us again so shot off again, and that's how it went for another ten minutes. Until it was tired out enough for Captain Kirk to slip a rope around its head.

"The stupid hook is caught in the stupid rope!" he yelled.

Hearing this, the garfish rolled, tore the rope right out of his hand, and shot off again for another run. But I brought it back, and the rope was still hooked by the hook, which the captain grabbed and began to untangle. Then he did some jimmy-rigging, wrangled a noose on the other end, and slipped it over its head. He got the rope under the pectoral fins, pulled it tight, and using one foot to hold the rope to the flat of the boat, yanked that gar head out of the drink. Then twisting the hook out of its gill, he threw all his weight into his shoulders, pulling that thing right into the boat. Meanwhile, the catfishermen watched on agape.

The gar, of course, smacked around, but Captain Kirk cranked back on the throttle and the engine lifted the front end up. The gar slid back, he caught it with his foot, pinned its head to the bottom of the boat, and we planed on back to the spot across from where the poles were set and broke out the measuring tape.

"Seventy-seven inches," Captain Kirk announced, "six-foot-five!"

Then he measured the girth and broke out his cell phone and started calculating with some sort of chart, because he left the scale in his other boat.

"One hundred and six pounds," he said. "She'd be fifteen more with her eggs, but it looks like she jettisoned them."

Before we could take any pictures, though, another squeal went off, so we shot back to the other side and Hippy grabbed the rod. This fish was going upstream, which was quirky and unusual. Pretty soon, however, it switched directions and we began floating after it. Then we were back in the eddy and Hippy was up front reeling in the slack.

"Set It!" Kirk yelled, and Hippy did. Then he did it four more times, every time the captain yelled it. Hippy even set it an extra time just to make sure. That gar was hooked good!

Ten minutes later, it was coming up to the boat. We saw it take shape, almost as long as mine, but not quite as fat. Its eyes were locked on all of us.

"It's mouth is open!" Kirk shouted. "Watch Out, She's Gonna Jump!"

And it did—right at us, SPLOOOOSHing as it leapt, twisting and shaking and flaring its fins! It was shooting to get into the boat—to attack us! But KAA-THWAAAACK—it hit the side. Then splashing all over the place, it was back in the river and taking out line.

Hippy was cheering, I was cheering, Captain Kirk was cheering, and so were the guys fishing for cats. Until, that is, Hippy brought the gar back and Kirk lassoed it and hauled it into the boat, where it flopped around, five feet long and forty-five pounds.

"A Double!" Captain Kirk cried—meaning two fish at the same time— just as I finished shooting my roll of film. So I rewound, took it out, and in the confusion, loaded it right back into the camera, thinking it was new.

Which is why the film also came out a double—as in "double exposed" —with eerie phantom gar-apparitions ghosting over pictures of family and friends. Luckily, though, the money shots came out.

In the meantime, we were riding a wheelie back to the spot and rushing with adrenaline and our two big fish were lying in the hull looking like funny chubby dolphins. In fact, they were even smiling as they watched us like horses, or dogs, or any sentient beings with eyeballs rotating in their heads.

"You boys get up in the front," Captain Kirk said as soon as he beached the bow on the mud where a water moccasin was flicking its angry tongue at us. But we didn't pay any attention to it, because we were getting up there and taking off our shirts, so as not to get all slimed up by gar goo.

Then the captain brought us our fish, hogtied in the hoisting rope. As soon as they were settled in our arms, their weight held them there. They didn't even fight, which was weird because all they had to do was snap their tails, knock us into the Trinity, chortle out some gar-giggles, and jump back in.

But they were chilling, because Captain Kirk had gar-whispered them. And though it's ridiculous to think that a fish could actually trust a human, that's what the scene was. In fact, they were still grinning as we cradled them, as if putting in time, knowing that we'd let them go if they played our game.

And as the Captain took a bunch of pictures, I checked out my mammoth gar, the one I had always tried to catch and finally did: the Lunker Six-Footer of all those kid-dreams, adult-dreams, thirty-something years of gar-dreams! Right there in my arms!

That's when I noticed a crevice running down its head, from beneath its eyes to the end of its snout. I guess I must've said something, because Captain Kirk immediately replied:

"That's the way they're built. They've got inter-locking plates."

And I was surprised, having no idea that their primitive skulls could be so complex.

Captain Kirk then pointed out some sea lice, which are these transparent dime-sized crustaceans that live on gar and eat their slime.

"Are they parasites?" I asked.

"Nope," he answered, "they're just harmless little bastards."

We also noticed a scrape running down my gar's back. It was about four feet long and the dentine of the armored scales was starting to grow back. The captain figured a prop had gouged it.

The author and Hippy and their double-exposed gars. Trinity River, Texas.
Photo courtesy of Mark Spitzer.

Then we let them go—our two beautiful goofy-looking fish.

And it didn't matter that Hippy and I only got two hours of sleep the night before, and it didn't matter that we should've been getting hungry for lunch, because we were flying high—all through the rest of the fishless day, into the evening, and then the night. Because we had just experienced "The Fishing Adventure of a Lifetime," just like the captain promised us.

Once again, he picked us up at 5:00 a.m., then took us to another spot—more downstream and bayou-like. There were levees on both sides and cattle grazing all around. Plus, there were nutria and beavers and cattle egrets and even a good old-fashioned eagle in the sky. But mostly, there were mosquitoes.

And "baby gar," as Captain Kirk kept calling them. They were swimming near the weeds by the bank, and since he had brought a dip net along, we occupied ourselves with catching them all day: longnose gar, spotted gar, and jet-black alligator gar spawn with bright gold racing stripes running down their backs. We caught a whole bucketful while waiting for the alarms to screech.

"Come On, Ladies!" the Captain kept calling out. "The Buffet Line's Closing Up!"

But the alarms never peeped and eventually we all fell asleep tied to the bank in the shade: Hippy in a lawn chair by the bow, me in the middle, Kirk in the stern, and no gar came along. It was just too cold from the floodwaters coming down.

So at two o'clock we shut it down, screamed on back to the launch, and got dropped off at the Motel 6. After which, Hippy and I bought a minnow-bucket aerator, and hit the highway up to Dallas.

"We got to keep our eyes out for the Feds," I told Hippy.

"Feds?" he asked. "Why?"

"Because we're transporting contraband gar across state lines," I replied. "There's got to be a law against that. In fact, there is a law against that."

"What law?" Hippy asked.

"The Lacey Act," I shot back, not knowing jack. "It has something to do with illegally introducing species, or unlawful stocking, or something like that. It was originally designed for tigers and rhinocerii, but then zebra mussels came along. It's all about keeping native species in their place."

"Well, that's bogus," Hippy said, "because aren't gar native to the whole dang continent?"

"Yeah, fossils from Kansas to the Arctic tell us this, but we can't tell the Feds that. We can't tell them, 'Sorry officer, we've got Gar Fever!'"

"Maybe," Hippy laughed, "we can tell them we're like Johnny Appleseed! Nobody ever busted him with the Lacey Act!"

Then up in Oklahoma, we were back in the rain, which was continually filling ditches and creeks and ravines in the state, then draining straight into Texas. That's when a cop pulled us over for doing eighty in a seventy, then gave us a warning and sent us on. Then another cop stopped us outside of Claremore, because my license-plate light wasn't working. But at least they didn't give us any guff about the forty or fifty gar-spawn in the back—because the gar-gods were still smiling on us.

By the time we got to Kansas City, the floods were really taking their toll. It was "Deluge!" on the radio. "Deluge Deluge Deluge Deluge! Head for the Hills!"

We stopped at a city park, however, and that's when the sun came out and we dumped our bucket into the Missouri River, thereby reintroducing an extirpated species into the upper Mississippi, and maybe even the Great Lakes.

Yep, with no consideration whatsoever as to what is legal or desired by the gar-fearing masses, we imposed our beliefs on millions that the big ones should return to the waters where they used to swim—tens of thousands of years ago, hundreds of thousands of years ago, a hundred million years ago! So that Midwestern Huck Finns like us can fish for them and not catch them and then catch them and ogle them and commune with them like generations have been doing for millennia.

"Because they're fantastic!" I told Hippy, standing there on the riverbank. "And misunderstood. And wiped out like the tribes of Israel, Africa, the Americas. But it's not too late to preserve what's been here longer than us, and the history of our consciousness."

That's how I tried to justify the breaking of a bogus eco-law, which probably isn't so bogus at all. Because if anything's bogus—

"It's the urge to smear our ancestors," I ranted on, being the bleeding-heart gar-liberal that I am, "who crawled from the muck almost 400 million years ago, so we could evolve into this!"

"So what you're telling me," Hippy said, "is that we are gar . . ."

"Sure," I returned. "But even if we're not, it's a self-destructive thing to crucify them for our sins when they've got a lot to offer. I mean, young gar feed on mosquito larvae. If we didn't run them out of most of the states, we'd have a lot less West Nile to deal with now. In fact, the first thing we should do after Third World populations get hit by hurricanes is stock their flooded streets with gar, to cut down on the waves of malaria that always follow. Plus, they'd make an excellent food source for starving masses ravaged by floods, who probably aren't so picky about the way a fish looks."

"Yeah," Hippy said, "maybe if we weren't so fat over here, we wouldn't be so quick to waste all that good meat."

"Seriously! There's a whole different attitude in Mexico. People are actually gar-farming down there and raising them for food. And here we are up here, allowing a bunch of doughy overfed yahoos to go into the spawning grounds and shoot them for 'sport.'"

"What a bunch of Stupids!" Hippy put in.

Then hopping back on I-35, we drove home at a reasonable speed— two "homegrown eco-terrorists" in the eyes of Homeland Security—and just as righteous as all the rest.

Or so the legend goes.

10

Frankengar

IN THE FIFTY-GALLON TANK to the left of the TV swims a hybrid gar. I've had it for seven years, it's twenty inches long, and it's twice the circumference of a bratwurst. It was once tiger-striped in silver and black, but now it's completely black.

Back in 2003, I used to get on eBay and do searches with the word "garfish." My hope was to find some beaten up old seven-footer that'd been mounted on a fifty-five-gallon drum of toxic waste someone was trying to get rid of. I figured I'd bid twenty bucks, win the thing, then drive across the country to get it. But that's not what I discovered.

A listing for "crocodile garfish" came up, which I had never heard of before. So I sent the seller a message asking what they were, and he replied that he ran a hatchery down in Florida and had crossed alligator and longnose gar and this is what he called them. He didn't know much about them, though, because basically the species just got invented. Still, he estimated that if longnose can reach six feet, and if alligator gar can get ten feet long, their offspring could grow to be somewhere in between. They cost $7.50 a piece, and he also had shortnose and longnose for $5 each.

I got on PayPal and sent him $17.50 pronto, plus shipping. Three days later a box arrived. And in that box was a plastic bag filled with water. And in that water was one purply shortnose, one silvery belly-up longnose, and a highly aggressive crocodile gar—all of them three inches long.

I put both survivors in a ten-gallon tank, which the hybrid soon ruled. It was crotchety and twitchy, always snapping at its own reflection, sometimes even sparring with it, while hogging all the food for itself.

Maybe, I thought, the shortnose was just more lethargic. Or, I considered, perhaps it got brain damaged from being shipped by the U.S. Postal Service. But whatever the case, I decided to separate them so the shortnose could get some grub.

The shortnose, however, just sat there like some sort of bummed-out fish on Prozac, not really caring if it got fed or not. Eventually I named it Scrawwww!, because a colleague asked me what its name was and I decided to screech out the sound of a crow.

Within a year, Scrawwww! died from depression, leaving me with just one gar: a totally demented mutant gar—which, with any sudden sound or movement in the room, would go bashing around the tank like a blind, deaf-and-dumb kid covered in fire ants.

And years later, it's still freaking out, always striking and striking and striking the glass—if not dancing in front of its own reflection, trying to taunt itself into a fight.

But mostly it just floats there in the plants beneath the fluorescent bulb.

At first I fed it grasshoppers caught in the yard, or crickets from the pet store. I'd drop one in and the flailing insect would attract the gar, who'd come up with its peripheral vision, then strike sideways, missing half the time. But when it hit, that bug was dead meat!

I also fed it little sunnies, bass, and random minnows caught at the lake. I'd drop them in and they'd huddle together, while the gar hovered above like a lance, snout pointing down, poised at a forty-five-degree angle, its rippling tail moving it back and forth with subtle undulations.

When that hybrid got to be about seven inches long, I switched its diet to night crawlers, which were an easier gar food to keep around, since there's always a carton in the fridge. But it wasn't easy getting it accustomed to worms. At first I'd drop them in and they'd sink to the bottom, where that gar, for some reason, refused to eat them. After a few weeks, though, I began to hold them on the surface, so they'd dangle and attract the gar. Who'd sidle up and then erupt, thrashing like a frothing hyena shaking its prey to break its neck.

This resulted in quite a few needly fangs sinking into my finger flesh before I got the hang of it. Once it even leapt from the tank and chomped on to my thumb, causing me to flick my hand back, launching it across the room. It landed on the carpet and I scooped it up with my bare hands—which I've done a couple times since then, and have never been bit. The only time it ever draws blood is when I'm feeding it and fail to move fast enough.

For the next few years, the hybrid would always wait on the surface for me to drop a night crawler in, which would get snatched the moment it hit the water. An epic battle would then ensue, with the crawler wrapping around the gar's jaws, fighting back like a giant squid. In the end, the gar always horked it down, before settling on the bottom to digest its one worm per day.

I was trying to stunt its growth, so it wouldn't grow ten to fourteen inches per year like they do in the wild. So it could hover there, lonely and exotically, all riled up for my amusement.

Until the day we move into a place with a swimming pool, I figured. At which point there will undoubtedly be a raging debate between my wife and me as to whether we're going to have pool parties with inflatable dinosaurs, or a six-foot-long monster fish snarfing down whole chickens.

My thesis, of course, will be that we can swim with the gar if we teach it to share its turf with people when it's small. Realistically, though, there's no way she'll go for this, and I'm not so sure I'd feel very comfortable skinny dipping with that thing, since I've seen what it can do to a worm.

And speaking of dismemberment, that gar is no stranger to laceration. For a while, it lived with a crayfish friend, which one day we discovered wasn't its friend, judging from the missing half of a pectoral fin.

That crawfish got demoted to bait, and then something phenomenal happened: The gar grew its fin back—which I later found out wasn't the first time this gar-trait had been observed. As the celebrated ichthyologist E. W. Gudger noted in a 1909 *American Naturalist* article titled "Notes on Some Beaufort Fishes," regarding two "shell gar" (or longnose) in North Carolina: "[T]heir pectoral and caudal fins were badly split and were congested with blood as a result of their threshing around on the floor of the boat during the journey of more than an hour from the fishing ground to the laboratory. Further, in a short time the fins of the living fish became much worn by contact with the scaling paint of the tank. . . . [But later] I found that the fish had completely regenerated their fins and that these were in as good physical condition as the day, then months before, when the gars were taken out of the bunt of the seine."

Still, my gar remains nameless. Sure, my colleague likes to refer to it as Not Scrawwww!, and I sometimes call it Garry Gordon (the vice president at our university), but much to my wife's consternation (she believes all pets should be named ASAP), I refuse to label it.

Because it's a freak! Yep, a bastard fish whipped up in some mad scientist's hatchery. And like all creatures condemned to live in hatred of themselves, I think it's only natural for it to lack the trappings of identity.

And so it continues its vicious existence, smacking and smacking and smacking the tank, while I cringe and cringe as it charges itself, flaring its nostrils at itself, refusing to accept the fact that it is alone in this world— a nameless, loveless, lone wolf confined to two cubic feet of space, dream-

Hybrid gar. Photo courtesy of James Cianciola, 2006.

ing of escaping into some lake. Where devouring ducks and gulping geese, it will seek its vengeance on anything that moves, especially humans, for making it a furious living thing, always Gnashing Gnashing Gnashing Gnashing at the glass.

In its older age, however, my gar started calming down. After we transported it to Arkansas in a giant tub, I changed its menu to an all-fish diet. It was about a foot long and its environment had been upgraded to a twenty-gallon tank, in which I installed "the cell of death"—a small netted enclosure in the corner meant for breeding guppies—but I kept feeder goldfish in it. That gar would hover there all day, watching its doomed food like a stalker.

What I found was that it preferred goldfish to night crawlers, or for that matter, anything. Sometimes I threw in small crappies, or bluegills I caught in my minnow trap. The hybrid, however, never went there—not if it didn't have to. It was much more partial to the soft scales and fins of the goldfish and trotline shiners I dropped in. In fact, that gar chose to live in peace with catfish and bass. When it was offered the choice between game fish and minnows, it always went for the latter.

More importantly, though, when I weaned my gar of night crawlers, it went through a major attitude adjustment. It stopped fighting itself, freaking out at the slightest movement, and generally, became a lot more resigned to its imprisonment.

So I upgraded its tank again, this time to thirty gallons. I even threw in a small gator gar I netted in Texas and had raised in another tank. The gator gar was half the size of the crocodile gar, and they got along fine. But then, one day, the gator gar just up and died.

Maybe it was the tail rot.

I had phased out the cell of death, and was keeping a bunch of gold-fish in a ten-gallon tank. Sometimes some would die, so rather than just throw them away, I'd toss them in the gar tank. The moment they hit the water, the hybrid would snatch them up. But if they settled on the gravel, it'd leave them alone, no doubt due to it's longnose genes. Whereas alligator gar are scavengers, longnose only go for live food.

Then one night, Robin took pity on a certain goldfish. She asked me to throw it in with her fancy goldfish, Goldy Extreme, so I obliged.

The next day, that new goldfish was all moldy, and we could clearly see that Goldy Extreme had caught some type of fungus. In a few days, both goldfish died.

A week later, I decided to surprise Robin by sneaking a new fancy goldfish into the empty tank. I was hoping the ick had gone away, but it hadn't. The new goldfish started croaking.

So we went out and got some tail-rot medicine and started treating the tank. Eventually, the new fancy goldfish made a full recovery, but not without coming out all black around the edges. In the meantime, my gar, who'd eaten a few contaminated goldfish, had lost all its chrominess and had turned almost completely black.

If that croco-gar got infected by the tail rot, though, I guess it fought it off. It never slowed down, never lost its balance, and never got leprosy in any of its fins. It just turned black as death.

Northern snakeheads, which gar are related to, have also been known to darken over time. As Eric Jay Dolin notes in his book *Snakehead: A Fish Out of Water* (2003), "captive northern snakeheads dramatically alter their color, going from pale, with bars and splotches, to very dark brown (nearly black)."

I've seen this happen to other aquatic creatures, but it usually happens in a chameleon-like way. For instance, when I introduced a muddy-colored siren (an eely salamander with mud-puppy gills) into another tank with Glummy Glummerson (a spotted gar), the siren became more yellowish and spotty, like the gravel. This seems to happen to bullheads as well, and other small fish I add and subtract from my various aquariums.

Still, there was nothing in the hybrid's environment that would've prompted it to change color. So I decided it was the Great Tail Rot Plague of 2008 that made my gar go to the dark side.

A week later, however, my friend the fish-and-wildlife writer Keith "Catfish" Sutton came over, took one look at that gar, and immediately diagnosed it as a male going through its spawning colors. This made a lot of sense, because the change began in April when the wild gar started spawning in the marsh by our yard. I felt like a fool, of course, for being so sure that tail rot had been the culprit, but I was glad to have the mystery solved.

Then two days later, just as suddenly as that gar turned black, it went back to its regular silveriness. Now, the only black it has on it are its tiger stripes. About two or three times per year, though (and mostly in the summer), he'll turn black for two or three weeks.

Since knowing this gar, I've learned that hybrids sometimes occur in the wild. Captain Kirk has caught a few in the Trinity River, and there are images on the Internet.

But if I've learned anything from watching my nameless gar (beyond the fact that gar avoid eating game fish), it's that gar make excellent pets. It's always entertaining to feed them in the presence of guests, and they're extremely low maintenance. They hardly poop, so you never have to change the water, and they get along well with other creatures.

Except that siren, who got a chunk of its tail bit off when I tried to make it live with the croco-gator gar. I should mention, however, that that siren now lives with Glummy in the tank below, and that they cuddle up together in the winter, as gar are prone to do.

Another thing I learned is that there's a lot of people out there who are quick to state that you can't keep gar, because they will quickly outgrow their aquariums. It's also been maintained that if you stunt their growth, they'll live a sickly existence.

This is complete baloney. As my gar can attest, if you feed it a minnow or two per day (enough to put a bulge in its belly), it can survive for years. It'll retain its spots of youth, which usually fade after the first season, and it'll stay healthy as long as it gets regular sunlight or fluorescence (a ten-watt bulb is enough). There should also be at least an inch of space above the surface, so it can come up and gulp air.

Meanwhile, my Frankengar still likes to spar with its reflection. But for the most part, its anger seems to be appeased. Until, that is, about nine o'clock every night. That's when it starts ramming the lid and dancing in the tank.

This means it's dinner time.

Gar in the Balance

Texas, the Trinity, and the Homosexual Rod & Reel

I WAS IN MY '93 Jeep Cherokee and cruise-controlling down to Texas at seventy miles per hour to meet a film crew from Animal Planet for a show they were making on alligator gar. They found me on the Internet and had commissioned me to play the role of some gar-nut. Or gar-enthusiast. Or gar-scholar, gar-writer, gar-advocate, whatever. We'd been talking on the phone and volleying e-mails all summer long so, now that it was early October, I had canceled my classes to actually get paid for fishing for gar. And talking about their issues. And bringing the bait.

Behind me in tow was the *Lümpabout*, a really *lümpen* 1959 runabout motorboat. It was a fifteen-footer with Batmobile fins, and had been sunk in a lake for ten years, but I had hauled it out, constructed a transom, reinforced the deck with two-by-fours, re-fiberglassed the whole thing, and given it a stripy green-and-yellow paint job. With that V-shaped hull, though, and that long-shaft 18-horse always hitting stumps, it wasn't very practical for garfishing the Trinity.

But that didn't matter, because I was determined to do it. After filming and fishing with Animal Planet, I figured I'd take it out on my own for some into-the-wild type man-vs.-gar action—so I kicked it up to seventy-five.

When I got to the Big Woods hunting lodge near Palestine, the whole British film crew was off filming humungo gar at the Texas Freshwater Fisheries Center in Athens. I had planned on arriving early, though, so I could try my new gar-gear out.

There was a public access off U.S. 287, which is where I went, then dropped it into four-wheel drive, because the launch was steep and covered in mud. Not only that, but the concrete ran out six feet before the swirling murk, and after that it was just giant chunks of cement and a pretty intense current.

As I backed on down, the excitement I had previously felt instantly turned to something like dread, since I was asking for trouble and I knew it. I mean, here I was dropping a fifty-year-old craft into a river full of rubble, where I'd be depending on a forty-four-year-old Johnson outboard.

Anyway, when the boat started floating off the trailer, I threw the tranny into park, cranked back on the emergency brake, jumped out, and slipped on the mud. My nervousness then changed to panic as I fell down and slid all over while pushing that sucker into the river. Still, I managed to pull the bow up on the bank and get my Jeep back up to the lot.

Then running back down and hopping in, I was floating downstream, yanking that rip cord and bonking rocks, but finally I got it going. "YEEEE-HAWWW!" I pointed upriver and throttled back. The front end lifted and suddenly I was cutting upstream and kicking up a wake, carving arcs between the deadheads and river snags, the muddy banks rising on both sides—thirty, forty, fifty feet high.

It was already dusk when I found the spot: a quarter-mile river bend with a sandbar on one side and eroding clay cliffs on the other. So I cut the power and drifted toward the deeper side, where the current was lazy. Then throwing out my cinderblock anchor, I started rigging up.

On my old gar rod with a bait-casting reel strung up with hundred-pound test and a mammoth treble hook, I stuck a one-foot grass carp. I'd bought thirteen of these at a fish farm out of Little Rock for two bucks a shot, and immediately iced them—literally. That is, I threw them live into a cooler, then dumped a bag of ice on top. Driving back, I knew they were gasping back there, and I knew I was becoming soft.

These days, every time I hook a minnow on one of my lines out in the lake (and I do this ten times per day), I find myself wincing. Which is something I never used to do, my logic always being: That's just the food chain, dude.

But that's stuff you can't think about or else you become some sort of vegan. So I cast that out, then grabbed my new rod: a heavy-duty salmon troller with a big black surf-sized spin-casting reel equipped with two-hundred-pound woven test. I stuck a bright orange koi on that (I'd bought ten for a dollar a piece), then cast that giant goldfish out.

With both baits settled on the bottom and their oversized cigar-shaped floats marking their locations (and providing me with something to chase if a gator gar went for my bait), I rigged up a lighter rod, this one with a night crawler on. And as soon as that settled on the bottom, the frogs starting chirping and glurphing and blurping away. The chorus rose and the skeeters came out—little black needly ones that evaded every swat. Luckily, though, I had a can of Off, so I sprayed myself down and kicked back in the stern.

A big gar rolled not too far away. By the size of its splash, it had to be a six-footer. Then I saw one surface. It was a thick gray seven-footer! They were definitely in this hole.

That's when my cell phone rang. It was the production assistant, who told me they were running late because Jeremy, the show's host, was swimming with a two-hundred-pounder and they were shooting footage. "No problem," I told her, because now I had more time to fish. She said we'd meet up later.

But after an hour out there, huge ones slapping all around and not getting anything, the sun started going down. I only had twenty minutes of light left, so I reeled in the lighter rod, and there was a painted turtle on it.

"Ha!" I laughed at it, working out the hook and tossing it back.

Then hauling in my other lines, I tore on back to the launch, cutting through swarm clouds of nymphs. At one point I hit a log and the motor popped up, but I kept on going, trying to keep my distance from the stumps. They were sticking up all around me and invisible beneath the murk.

I made it, though, and pulled up on the scree, which cost me some fiberglass. Then backing my Jeep down the launch, I got the *Lümpabout* on the trailer, pulled out, cranked down the straps, and shot back to the lodge, glad that I didn't have to call the sheriff to come out and rescue me—or even worse, that I didn't have to wait all night for some fisherman to find me, thereby missing my rendezvous with the film crew. Who, no doubt, expected a professional—not some clumsy amateur.

Back at the ranch, I cracked a Guinness and took a seat in a giant rocking chair made from rustic logs, and was immediately dwarfed by the furniture—which, I figured, was made for XXL Texans. There were mountain goat heads and deer busts on the walls and photographs of funny-looking long-necked birds.

Since I'd gotten up at six that morning and hadn't had much to eat, and since it was getting on eleven, it didn't take long before I fell asleep. Ten minutes later, though, I heard gravel crunching and car doors closing. Before I could get up, they burst on in with their booms and mics and packs of gear: the cameraman, the sound guy, the director, the production assistant, and then, of course, Jeremy.

Jeremy Wade was the star of the show. A wiry white-haired bespectacled guy about fifty years old, he was a freelance-writer-turned-fishing-show host. As an "extreme angler," he was famous for traveling all over the globe, catching mega-Mekong cats in Asia, leviathan-lunkers in the Amazon, and bull sharks in South Africa. Jeremy had written me a few years back about the idea of doing a show on "man-eating gar," and now it was happening.

Someone plopped a case of Coronas down and we helped ourselves. I liked them all, but connected with Jeremy the most, because instantly, we started talking gar. He'd caught two so far in the four days they'd been here: One was a five-foot fifty-pounder, and the other one had been six-foot-seven, one hundred twenty-six pounds. But the thing is, they caught it at night, so they didn't get a very good shot.

Then we started talking gear. Jeremy had been using wire leaders, but I'd come from the school of Captain Kirk, who didn't use leaders at all: just straight-up braided line. Jeremy, however, had decided to switch to a three-foot-long Kevlar leader meant for monster fish in Thailand, which was highly flexible and braided as well, so it wouldn't cut a fish's mouth.

The others went out to smoke and Jeremy and I kept talking methods and equipment. We talked fishing line and floats, and then we got to hooks. I had brought a bunch of oversized trebles, because that's what most gator-gar fishermen have always used. But Jeremy felt that those two extra barbs upped the chances that the fish would sense something steely and drop the bait, so he was rigging up a large circle hook, which he figured would slip into the corner of a gar's mouth. He reasoned it was better for the gar to use a single rather than a triple, because if you can't get the hook out, a single barb would do less damage.

Anyway, they were beat, I was beat, so eventually, we all went to sleep.

At seven in the morning (not five, thank God!), I got up and went down and met Bubba, who was not a burly three hundred pounds. He was a tall, skinny Texan in Wranglers and cowboy boots, about thirty years old with a tough young Republican haircut. We shook hands.

Bubba was the captain of the airboat the crew had been using for the last few days, as well as the owner of the land they'd been launching on. Bubba's family owned two thousand acres adjacent to the Trinity on a rarely traveled section of the river. He was a bowhunting guide who ran an outfit called Garzilla, and he catered to an elite crowd of garchers that paid $1,250 per day per person to shoot sixty-year-old eight-footers. Bubba had grown up hunting bucks and killing gar on the Trinity. He didn't think much of angling, but was glad to be involved in the show.

Bubba and I went over to the main house, met the film crew, and sat down for a Texas-sized breakfast. It'd been a long time since I'd seen three slices of bacon on my plate, plus two eggs over easy, rolls the size of softballs, and coffee. After that, we were on our way.

I rode with Bubba, who immediately asked me what my deal was. I told him I was a garologist.

"Like a professor of gar?" he asked.

"Yeah," I told him. "I write about gar and ecology. I research gar history, gar folklore, gar science, and I fish for them as well."

This immediately put Bubba on the offense. Before I knew it, he said flat out:

"You don't like bowhunters!"

By the tone of his voice, I could tell that the division between anglers and bow fishermen was something he took more personally than most. A long awkward silence ensued, in which I considered how my conflict with bowhunters mostly existed in my head, because I never meet them. I just see the fish they toss away and complain about how gar are treated. Bubba, however, was in the thick of it, dealing with bowhunters all the time. Or customers, or clients, or whatever you want to call them. Meanwhile, there's been a controversy brewing in Texas over protecting alligator gar from guys like the "Gar Guys," who take big-dollar trophy hunters into the spawning grounds and shoot 'em up like no tomorrow.

Anyway, hoping humor could work as some sort of peace offering, I broke the silence by answering:

"I like you, Bubba."

"You better," he responded, "or I'll kick your ass right out of this truck!"

I laughed, but only so he wouldn't be embarrassed.

"Let me tell you why it's okay to kill them gar," Bubba said, then went into a speech on how people in these parts have always killed gator gar and will always kill gator gar and it's alright because there are thousands of them in these rivers and creeks and reservoirs and ponds, and you just can't kill them off.

Of course, I didn't tell Bubba that this we've-got-more-than-we-need mentality is what led to the wiping out of the big ones in Arkansas, thanks to guides cashing in on populations depleted by dams and insecticides. And I also didn't add that Texas's recent boom in gator gar hunting is the exact same thing that happened in Arkansas back in the '50s, so it would be really stupid and self-destructive to not look at the mistakes made in that state, then apply those lessons to what's going on today.

Instead, I just sat there and listened to him tell me about a four-mile-long lake on his land with a mongo albino in it, a ten-foot gar that's got to be a world record. His plan was to let it get bigger, then take it down and get the record.

Bubba also had a theory that gar grow bigger in muddier waters because they can't see what they're eating, so they eat all the time. This didn't make much sense to me, but I kept on listening.

He knew the Gar Guys, but didn't much care for them. They had actually gotten him into the gar-guiding business. After hearing how they were making money on shooting gar, he offered them access to his stretch of river and had gone out with them to see how they ran their business. Bubba learned from them and every time they took a client out from his land he'd get a cut. But then the Gar Guys started bringing more and more bowhunters up and killing more and more big gar, and Bubba wasn't seeing his cut, so he told them they couldn't come up anymore and now they don't talk anymore.

"I realized I could make some bucks," Bubba stated, "so I started a business of my own."

I asked him what he did with the big ones his customers shot, and he told me that most of them got mounted. As for the ones he shot himself, he just dumped them on his land. The Gar Guys, on the other hand, were commercial fishermen, who, Bubba claimed, sold their meat to Long John Silver's, which chopped it up and mixed it into fish burger.

We then drove by some penitentiaries and arrived at Bubba's place on a tributary of the Trinity. It was a shack on sticks, eight feet off the ground, with peeling paint and a Coors Lite sign on the porch.

"C'mon," Bubba said, getting out and leading me to the bank, where he had a trammel net full of buffalo. Some were dead, some were alive.

I had brought a bunch of buffalo myself, which I got from this guy who runs a fish market in Mayflower, Arkansas. Thirty-six pounds for eighteen bucks.

For the last few days, Jeremy's crew had been working with a guide named Mick, who, I was told, never shut up. But now Mick was gone. Originally, I was going to be the guide, and we were going to fish down by Huntsville in the area I'm familiar with. I was sort of relieved, though, when my role changed from gar-guide/gar-know-it-all to that of just gar-know-it-all, because then I wasn't under pressure to produce the fish.

But now, with the absence of Mick, Bubba had appointed himself guide as well as captain. This didn't bother me at all, but I was miffed when he told me we didn't need my bait, because his was fresher. I'd been told to bring an assortment, because then I could talk to Jeremy about our choices, and they could film us trying out different fish. The director's assistant was particularly interested in the sheepshead I said I'd bring.

Anyway, I wasn't going to argue with Bubba, but I wasn't going to leave my bait behind. As I helped him load his buffalo up, it was clear that he was alpha. Then he went and got two fresh hog livers from some wild boars he shot the night before, plus a dead squirrel in a plastic sack.

"Them gar'll eat anything," he told me, asserting his authority—because he's the guy who grew up hunting them, and I'm just some academic who reads *Lepisosteus* studies.

Then the film crew showed up in two white rental vans. I hopped in Bubba's truck and he led our convoy through the woods and along a field, bouncing over ruts and bumps while deer went bounding through the bloodweed.

Down on the river, there was an airboat tied up. It was twenty-something-feet long with a 454 Chevy engine with a raised Edelbrock manifold and a 750 four-barrel carb bored out to 900 and no mufflers whatsoever.

"Gets one mile per gallon," Bubba bragged.

We loaded all the stuff and got in. The sound guy then clipped mics on Jeremy and me, and Bubba handed us some headphone-looking ear-protection things and got up in his high-up throne and fired up the V8. The prop spun and it roared to life, rattling our teeth and esophogi.

Herons and egrets screeched for cover as the airboat tore upstream, sending out a three-foot wake as we flew over snags and logs and strips of beach like a pack of combusting Harleys. We went five miles in less than ten minutes, burned up twenty bucks worth of gas, and got to a spot where Bubba said there were seven-footers.

Jeremy and I baited up, and as we did, we talked about the bait and the cameraman filmed away. Jeremy chose half a bowfin I brought along, and I cut up one of Bubba's buffalo for myself. Then I showed Jeremy the grass carp and koi, a spare tilapia, half a drum.

"And I hear you have something mammalian?" Jeremy asked in his British accent.

"I do?" I asked back.

"Yes," he prompted, "I heard you have a mammal of sorts . . ."

"Well, there's supposedly a dead squirrel," I offered cautiously, not so sure that the animal rights activists would appreciate seeing us hook up a rodent.

"No no," Jeremy said, "I heard you were bringing a sheep's head."

"We're backwards in Arkansas," I laughed at that, "but not that backwards. A sheepshead is a freshwater drum, sometimes called 'gou' in Louisiana."

Everyone got a kick out of that. They actually thought that I brought the head of a sheep to fish with! And that's not the only thing I said that they took literally, but we'll get to that in a bit.

We started fishing. Jeremy had one big chunk on the bottom and was floating another four feet beneath a giant bobber. He had a lot more line than me, which I soon found out was an advantage. My bait-casting reel had about a hundred yards of moss-green line, but it was a pain to hand-release. And the two-hundred-pound test on my new rod was so thick that my reel could only hold about a hundred yards as well. Meaning Jeremy was able to get his bait hundreds of yards downstream, but I was pretty much relegated to right beneath the boat, since I had to keep some line on to play a gar if one came along.

So we fished in that spot for about an hour and we didn't catch anything. In the meantime, downstream in the bend, we could see an occasional seven-footer (and even an occasional eight-footer) come up and roll.

Bubba said they stake out an area, and we could see that this was true. If a big gar rolled right next to a log, it'd come up again in the same spot twenty minutes later. They weren't moving up and down the channel at all, but they were moving. And as the sun rose higher, they rolled even more.

Bubba then told us that he could predict their rolls, because he had some sort of gar-sense. He also said that they'd only roll when the water was still. But whenever they rolled, I noticed that there were slight ripples on the surface, because low-lying clouds were coming through, pushing the wind ahead of them, causing hawks to spiral above. I'd seen this type of change in barometric pressure cause the shortnose to leap in Missouri, and now I was seeing the same thing again. I let Bubba have his moment, though, even though I knew he was wrong. I wasn't about to contradict him.

The way we were fishing was also quite different than the way I'd done it with Captain Kirk. Whereas Kirk talked loudly and banged around, and didn't caution his clients about making noise, Jeremy was completely opposite. He asked us all to talk in whispers, and told us to keep our movements to a minimum.

After a while, catching nothing, I suggested we move down to the bend where the big ones were rolling. I suggested this to Jeremy, because I figured if I said it to Bubba he'd resist me, just for the sake of resisting me. So Jeremy suggested we drift downstream, and when we got to the spot, I told Jeremy that this was the spot, and he told Bubba to stop.

It was a quarter past noon now and Bubba's daddy would be showing up with brisket at 12:30, but Jeremy wasn't fixing on rushing back. He told us we'd give this spot twenty minutes, then get back for lunch a little late. So as our stomachs grumbled, we baited up.

Jeremy's method was to scale his fish chunks, but only where the hook went through. He said this would ensure that the scales wouldn't get in the way of the hook. He also cut off the fins so that the tender flesh of the gar's mouth wouldn't get poked and cause the fish to spit it out. But I just hooked them under their spines, figuring these gar were used to crunching up fins.

Anyway, we weren't catching anything in that spot. They just weren't biting that day. Jeremy, however, said we'd stick it out for five more minutes.

That's when one of his reels started clicking. It was the floatless line, a hundred yards ahead of the boat. So as the cameraman sprang into action, I immediately reeled in both my lines. Because that's the Captain Kirk method: You get everything out of the water that can get tangled up, and you float down after the gar, constantly feeding out line until it stops. Then you reel in the slack and set the hook on its second run.

Jeremy hadn't gone after a gar like this before, but that's what we were going to do, because that's the method I told him was best. So Jeremy directed Bubba to untie the line, and we started drifting after it.

Jeremy then handed me his other rod, and told me to reel it in slowly. I replied that we should just get it out of there, but he said no, just take in the slack. This didn't seem practical to me, but I did as he said—and it's a good thing too, because five minutes later that float took off.

That float, however, was just too jumbo, and the gar could feel its resistance. After a minute it coughed up the bait and swam off. Meanwhile, we were getting closer and closer to Jeremy's fish, which had stopped to digest.

I got my line out of the way, and then Jeremy's gar started heading upstream. It passed the boat, the line went taut, and he hauled back, setting it good. WHAM! that gar shot upstream like a rocket.

Jeremy, however, horsed it in while I rustled up my special yellow hoisting rope. Having watched Captain Kirk haul them in with a primitive noose, I had innovated on this method by taking a length of rope and attaching a stainless steel metal clip that could take over two hundred pounds of stress. This way, I wouldn't have to tie any knots. All I'd have to do was get that rope around a gar, clip it, pull it, and haul it in—so I was ready to test my invention out.

The gar started heading toward the boat, which made it difficult for Jeremy. He had to reel in super fast, and then it was under the bow, thrashing like a crack baby, splashing everyone on board. A six-foot fatty at least, and mad as hell!

Jeremy thought he should let it make another run and tire it out because it was just way too fired up to bring into the boat at that moment. I agreed, but then Bubba stepped up:

"Give me that rope," he ordered me, and I did.

On one hand, I was upset that he was stealing my thunder, but on the other hand, I was relieved that it wouldn't be me getting filmed—because what if I screwed up?

Bubba leaned down, got the rope under the gar, slipped it under its pectoral fins, clipped the clip, and tightened up. Then hauling back, he lifted its head out of the river. It smashed around, and its head hit the hull with a resounding THWACK! Then Bubba hauled back again and pulled it up on the deck, where again it smashed around, lashing its tail like a raging dragon. And when the cameraman moved in for a close up, it smacked the camera right in the lens and shattered it.

I broke out the tape measure while the cameraman switched equipment. Bubba said something about watching out for its tail, but having dealt with big gar before, I ignored him. Plus, I was getting pretty tired of his competitiveness, when I was hired just like him to bring my experience to this trip.

"Eighty and a half inches," I said. "Six foot eight and a half."

Then the gar went wild again. I stayed out of its way, though, no problem.

"Can we get another shot of Mark measuring the fish?" the director asked.

So I kneeled down and did it again, holding the tip of the tape measure to the tip of the fish's nose. Bubba, however, had to get into the shot, so he grabbed the other end of the tape measure and took it down toward the tail.

"Seventy-nine inches," he said.

"Six-foot-seven!" somebody cheered, and that's the measurement that stuck.

I grumbled inaudibly, but let it go as Jeremy exchanged high fives and shook hands with everyone and the sound guy thanked Bubba for all he had done.

We then shot back to the launch, Jeremy pouring water on the gar to keep it wet. There was sea lice all over its armor. I flicked a few off and took a look at the spot where the gar had smashed its head against the hull. It was bleeding and bruised and the skin was cracked open like the rind of a cantaloupe someone had kicked, blood running out of it.

It really bummed me out, looking at that injury, the poor thing. And not only that: It had swallowed the hook, and now there was no getting it back. But again, that's something you can't dwell on, so I tried to put it out of my mind, knowing that its gastric acids would dissolve the metal eventually.

When we pulled up to the launch, Bubba's entire family was there. His boys came running down to see the fish, his father was carrying a baby, and Bubba's brother and wife were milling around and setting up lunch.

But first we had to weigh the gar and get some more shots. So we got it in a sling, put it on the scale, and the verdict was 111 pounds. Then we hauled it down to the beach and placed it in a few inches of water. Jeremy got behind the fish and talked to the camera about what a fight it put up, while the sound guy shot stills with a waterproof camera. In the meantime, Bubba was pacing back and forth, telling the director, "I want a picture, I want a picture, I want a picture!"

But the director wanted me in the shot, so she told me to go down there and get in it so that Jeremy and I could talk about the gar. I did, but then here comes Bubba, and he gets in there right between us, so the three of us lifted the fish. And as we did, I restrained myself from commenting on how ridiculous it is that we feel the need to hold it in our

Spitzer with Bubba Bedre, Jeremy Wade, and a six-foot-eight alligator gar caught on the Trinity River in Texas while filming an episode of the Animal Planet series *River Monsters*.

arms to prove that we conquered it. I mean, it's here, we've got it, so why must we be so obvious?

Jeremy then let the fish go, but it had trouble making it out to deep water. It kept swimming downstream parallel to the shore in five or six inches of water. It just couldn't make the turn, or its instincts were too confused, and then it just stopped, as if giving up. Jeremy, though, went after it, turned it around, and shoved it out to sea.

Then again I was feeling sorry for that gar. This feeling, however, instantly turned to anger at myself. What was wrong with me!? First, I question whether it's right to kill bait, then I feel sympathy for a big dumb fish! What will I do next? Pass up the barbecued beef and only eat the potato salad? Organize a million-gar march on Washington?

But, of course, I just went up there and ate my lunch.

Then it was time for my interview. I'd brought my garchives, and they were laid out on the picnic table: manuscripts, documents, books, pictures, studies, articles, all my stuff. Jeremy was sitting next to me, the camera was filming away, and Bubba and his daddy and the kids were sitting in lawn chairs watching "the Yankees" talking gar.

During lunch, Bubba's daddy had brought out a picture of an eight-foot-four-incher that Bubba and his brother had killed. It was 230 pounds and overflowing from the bed of a pickup. The head of that sucker was as big as Bubba's torso, as he stood behind it grinning like the Cheshire Cat.

"He don't like bowfishin'," Bubba had said to his daddy—which was the equivalent of him saying, "Don't show him that, he'll just get mad."

But I didn't. I'd been seeing pictures like this for years—it comes with the territory. And the trick, of course, is to not react when something disturbs you, especially when you need to get things done. Besides, I was open to being open to bowfishing, because I knew my bias was biased, and there were things I could learn from hanging around guys like Bubba.

Bubba, however, had turned to me as soon as his daddy walked away, and said, "I saw the look on your face when you looked at that picture. You was mad."

But like I said, I wasn't mad. If anything, I was bummed out—and I might've reflected a bit of that.

The point being: Bubba was watching me, and watching me closely. And now that I was getting interviewed, he was still watching me, so I was holding back on answering sincerely. Because what I was talking about was the decline in gator gar populations and how they're endangered throughout their range and how bowhunting and trophy-fishing is what wiped them out in Arkansas in just three years. And since the director wanted me to talk about this, I felt I had to find a place where I could give Animal Planet the information they wanted without provoking the wrath of Bubba and his daddy.

And to an extent, I found that place. I was able to talk about generations of hatred being leveled at the species, and people passing that hatred on to their kids. But in doing so, I set the blame more on the ignorance of state agencies and sloppy science rather than the settlers and fishermen who accepted the hearsay pumped up by the media.

I also talked about Col. J. G. Burr of Texas and his *Electrical Gar Destroyer*, which led to other forms of electrocution employed by conservation departments across the country to eradicate gar. The director wanted to hear about this, but she especially wanted to hear about this little girl in Mandeville, Louisiana, back in 1932.

The film crew had recently recreated this alleged attack, and the director was interested in getting to the bottom of this matter. She'd told me she'd read that the girl ended up with "a bloody stump," so they wanted to hear the details. But from everything I had read (and there's really no evidence that this actually happened), it seemed to me that her foot had only been mangled a bit.

That's when it hit me that I was the one who started the rumor of the bloody stump. Not that I intended to—but this is what happened: Back in 2002 I had a garticle published in which I was shooting off my mouth to my friend Kevin about this very incident, and in relaying the little girl story to him, I had shown myself spectacularizing the details. I wasn't lying when I wrote that I told Kevin that she emerged from Lake Pontchartrain with a bloody stump, because I really told Kevin that—so I was telling the truth in what I wrote.

When I mentioned earlier that these Brits took something else I said literally, this is what I was talking about. And this sort of thing is always an issue in creative nonfiction: where one draws the line between the truth of the matter and what gets embellished. As I tell my students, fiction is the realm of lies, whereas creative nonfiction is the realm of truth. In both, however, there's a crossover, which makes for the eternal question of the writer's intention versus the audience's expectations. It's a complex equation, and the questions never get answered to everyone's satisfaction—which is good for the genre, because it provides for a set of discussions on ethics that injects the discipline with an urgency that keeps it relevant and interesting.

Anyway, as I told Jeremy:

"Big fish make for big stories, and when it comes to gar, it doesn't take much for the details to become fantastic."

I then explained how there's a consistent history of distorting information when it comes to gar, and that I had made a study of how this misinformation has always been an active element in blowing the facts out of proportion.

In the end, though, Jeremy asked if the recent attention alligator gar have been getting from the media, and all the various studies in the works, has helped the species break into our consciousness, therefore helping them to survive. And my answer to this was:

"No. Gar still don't register on the mainstream radar as a creature worth preserving."

I then talked about how we know more about gar than we used to know, but that's only because we're being forced to. It's like global warming; we look for solutions because we have to, because it's there, and if we don't do anything about it, it's unconscionable.

"Meanwhile," I stressed, "the salmon fishery on the West Coast has completely collapsed, hundreds of thousands have just disappeared, and 70 percent of the world's sturgeon population has vanished in the last twenty years. Alligator gar could very well be the next to go."

I looked over at Bubba and his daddy. They were not amused.

Back on the river, Jeremy hooked up a big orange koi, I hooked a grass carp up, and even Bubba casted out.

"Maybe you'll make a fisherman out of me," Bubba joked. "I bet you'd like that, huh professor?"

By this time I'd had enough.

"I don't judge bowhunters," I lied. "I mean, I kill minnows every day. Why's the life of a big fish worth more than a little fish's?"

Bubba didn't respond. We just kept fishing. And turtles kept taking my bait.

After a bit, though, Jeremy's line took off. So we did the same thing we did before: went floating after while I reeled in Jeremy's other rod. And again, after his gar came to a stop, it started heading upstream.

Jeremy set the hook and it jumped. Just a three-footer, but a sleek, beautiful, pikey-looking fish, which nobody even had to rope up. Jeremy just lifted his rod and pulled it onto the deck.

"Well, we've learned something," Jeremy told the camera. "The smaller the bait, the smaller the fish."

I held it down and we checked it out. The hook was way down in its throat, so I got out a tool I'd brought along that holds a fish's mouth open. Jeremy stuck his pliers in and cut the Kevlar as far down as he could.

That's when the gar snapped back, spit the tool out, and leapt. It happened so fast that nobody even saw it, but it chomped onto Jeremy's hand and bit him hard. The next thing you know, he was bleeding all over the place.

"Score one for the gar," I said.

Jeremy let it go and someone broke out a first aid kit, then went about disinfecting the wound. The cameraman, however, declined to film this.

So we stuck it out till dark, not catching anything—which wasn't that surprising to me, since studies show that gator gar do most of their feeding before noon.

Bubba then fired up the prop and we roared back to the launch in a blazing cloud of halogen-illumed flies. It was like *Star Trek,* all those distant specks of light turning into sudden lines and zipping past at warp speed.

An hour later, riding with Bubba in the truck, we passed a wild hog on the side of the road. It was lit up in the headlights and looking hilarious with that big old head and skinny legs. I could see the tusks as well as its razory back.

We were heading back to the lodge to get ourselves a big Texas gar-getting dinner. And when we walked into the dining hall, the owner of the lodge was there, chowing down on fried chicken.

"Hey," he said when he saw us, "catch anything on those homosexual rods and reels?"

Bubba laughed but I didn't. I just headed for the buffet, got myself two drumsticks, a big splat of mashed potatoes, and poured the gravy on. Then pretty soon, the film crew came in and got their grub too.

After the cobbler, though, I couldn't help but notice the smell on my hands. I'd washed them twice since holding that last gar, but the scent of its goo was still there. It was an indescribable pungent smell that lay somewhere between rotting cardboard and all the biodegrading shellfish-shores I had ever hoofed in my life. It had a rife toxicity that couldn't be denied, nor washed off my flesh for at least three days.

The following morning I said my goodbyes to Jeremy and the crew, then lit out on my own, to get a gar of my own. This time, I was a lot less frantic lowering my boat into the river. Compared to the other day, this was a flawless surgery.

Then firing up my trusty outboard, I pointed upstream and cut through the curves, hitting an occasional under-log, but not enough to do more than toss the boat into a momentary wobble.

I passed the bend where I fished before and kept on heading upriver. Went about a mile, found a spot, took out the bait, and started fishing.

It was pretty much the same story as the day before, with all the big ones rolling downstream, and me floating my bait down to them as close as I could. A few times the bait got nabbed, but they spit it out pretty quickly. Which was okay, in a way, because I'd forgotten my special yellow yanking rope and I barely had enough line to let a gar make a run.

More than anything, this trip had been a learning experience. I never knew so much line was required, and I also found out that going for alligator gar is hardly recommended for just one fisherman. It takes one to fight the fish, and another to handle the boat. Running with Bubba, however, had also learned me a thing or two about the local attitude toward fishing with rod and reel, which I always suspected, but had never met face to face.

After an hour of getting sunburned, I tried another spot, this one on the edge of a slow swirling eddy. It was deep where I positioned the boat in the middle of the bend, so I dropped my bait right there, not more than twenty yards out.

Bubba claimed that you had to have a camouflaged hull, and that you have to hide in the shade, because if a gator gar sees your boat, it won't come near. But from fishing with Kirk and fishing on my own, I knew this factor wasn't that important. I'd caught plenty of gar in Arkansas not too far from my yellow-green canoe. I even caught the state record spotted gar (seven pounds) with a liver, right next to my canoe—but like an idiot, I'd thrown it back.

Anyway, it didn't take long for a gar to hit. Or maybe it wasn't a gar— I don't know. All I know is that the float went straight down. It didn't take off for the center of the river, it didn't trail a wake at all—just went straight down with a *Sploonk*ing sound.

Man, I was adrenalized! I fed out line and fed out line, and that float never came up. Whatever took it down must've been a big one, and it must've gone downriver, I figured, as I got out of the boat and followed it along the shore, still feeding it line.

It stopped a couple of times and so did I. And each time it stopped, I waited ten minutes, always restraining my inner-catfisherman, who was yowling for me to set the hook. But I didn't. I waited it out. And when it took off again, and I saw I only had a few yards left, I set it with a dramatic yank.

Nothing.

The float popped up right beside me, so I went back and tried it again. Still nothing.

Then, around noon, I headed back to that first bend where I'd fished the other evening by myself. There was just something about this spot. It was rolling with big gar and I knew it was deep. So I got out there on the edge of it and cast my bait into the outer limits of the eddy.

Three or four times, a lunker gar came along. My bait shot off every time, the line unspooled, and within minutes, I was down to my last few yards and forced to set the hook. It sucked that the bait kept popping out, but it was also a relief to know that I wasn't ripping up a gar's throat.

Once, though, I felt a moment of resistance. This was followed by a sudden eruption a few seconds later right where my bait had been. It was a frothing-mad seven-footer, splashing all manic and spitting out the bait, but making the whole day worthwhile.

Still, there was more gar action that afternoon. At one point, a gar took my float straight into my other float, got them all tangled up, and got off after I tried to set it. And another time, reeling in a chunk of buffalo, something suddenly took it down, right there under the boat. I fought it for a bit, and it was way heavier than the 106-pounder I caught with Captain Kirk. Then, just as suddenly as it struck, it was gone.

Which I decided I should be, since I still had six hours to drive and it was coming up on three o'clock. So I dumped my remaining bait in the river, thanked the gar for all that they had given me, and shot off downstream.

It took a while to get back to the launch, because I hit a log, the motor popped up, and when I revved it, there was no power to the prop. A shear pin had been broken, so I spent ten minutes fixing that, then shot off again—only to hit another log and bust another pin.

But an hour later, I was on the road, the *Lümpabout* trailing in my rearview mirror. And muddy and sunburnt and dehydrated, I couldn't help but give Bubba some credit.

That night when we saw the wild boar, he told me he thought the state laws would soon be changing for gator gar. I asked him why, and he replied that he felt the political push for it, and even agreed with the idea of setting a bag limit of one gar per year for fish over a hundred pounds to ensure that there'd be more big ones in the river for him and his clients. A special license for alligator gar, he also reckoned, would cut down on commercial fishermen like the Gar Guys taking as many as they can.

This admission had pretty much shocked me, because I thought I had Bubba pegged. Yep, beneath all that you-just-can't-kill-'em-off bravado, I had sensed a slightly effeminate fisherman who just might have some respect for the "homosexual rod and reel." Or, at least, I sensed a conservationist who knew these gar way better than most people on the river. And because of his true connection with them, he had to fess up that the supply wasn't as plentiful—or as sustainable—as he first suggested it was.

But whatever the case, I figured as I hit the interstate, if Texans are in charge of the last major population of alligator gars in the nation (and the world), then those big bad beautiful fish that Bubba and I love so much . . . well, they're definitely still in a whole lot of trouble.

12

Arkansas Gar Wrangling

Out of Sight, Out of Mind

AFTER BEING SWORN TO SECRECY, we took off for Arkansas's hottest gator-gar hole—which I'm not about to divulge. All I'll say is that a surprisingly large number of them was recently discovered, so now there's two known breeding populations in the state. The thing about this specific population, though, is that the flood plains and herbaceous vegetation in the spawning grounds still haven't been ruined by humans. And since hardly any bowhunters know about this spot, there's a chance that we can protect these fish and bring their numbers up. Which are calculated to be somewhere between seventy-five and a hundred alligator gar.

This figure is based on some sort of mark-recapture formula. By tagging individual gar, then releasing them and catching them later, biologists use the ratio of re-caught gar to never-tagged gar to come up with statistics. I'm not sure how it works, but that's what we're doing on this bone-numbing January morning. Our group is: Dr. Reid Adams of the University of Central Arkansas Biology Department, a quixotic ichthyologist collecting data so the Arkansas Game & Fish Commission can get some restrictions into place; Lindsey Lewis of the U.S. Fish and Wildlife Service, who's been doing this type of work for years and is the state record holder of the shortnose gar on rod and reel; Ed Kluender, a hippy-looking graduate student with dreadlocks and a power drill for the attaching of transmitters to track the movements of these creatures up and down the muddy river; J. P., the burly bearded bowhunter who brought this population to the attention of the Biology Department by shooting a 175-pounder a few years back; Tommy Inebnit, whose in-progress thesis has to do with aspects of reproductive ecology in this particular population; a recent UCA graduate named Richard Walker, who did a study on the diet of shortnose in this system and is now employed by Dr. Adams;

and the writing professor they let tag along, because I wouldn't stop bugging them to let me observe. They, however, intended to put me to work.

Needless to say, I was psyched. Last time this team went out, they caught fifteen big ones ranging from eighty to one hundred eighty pounds. Plus, their cutting-edge research was the talk of the 2008 *Lepisosteus* Conference recently held in New Orleans.

When we got to the launch, I was given a pair of plastic overalls, some fancy diving gloves, and a life jacket. I hopped into the "running boat" (a flat-bottomed craft with a forty-horse Mercury outboard) with J. P. and Tommy, and the others got into the U.S. Fish and Wildlife boat, which had a 150-horse and a lot more room for moving around. Both boats were full of giant holding tubs, baskets of nets, and floats galore. There was a collapsible shark-cage-looking thing on board the U.S. Fish and Wildlife boat, and the running boat was filled with weights made by pouring concrete into liter-sized soft drink containers.

We fired up the engines, took off, and I talked to J. P. as he drove. He worked in the university's physical plant, but on gar-getting days like these he'd go out to run nets, drive boats, provide guidance, and hang out with the biologists. He'd been bowhunting up and down this river for years and had all sorts of stories to tell. What impressed me the most, though, was that after he got that seven-footer a few years back, he didn't feel the need to bowhunt gator gar anymore. These days, he only goes out for buffalo and smaller species of gar because, like everyone else on this trip, he is committed to preserving the last of the big ones in the state.

We got to the first hole where, according to Ed's receiver, a transmitter-equipped gar had been "pinging" the night before. We started putting out the nets, which had three-inch mesh and were about a hundred feet long. The idea was to put one "block net" upstream and one downstream, then go "rodeoing" in between—which meant spinning donuts to scare the gar into the nets.

But before we finished spreading the nets, there was something so obvious that none of us could ignore it: J. P.'s slickers were all blown out in the back, and as he worked away, bending over and grabbing nets, he had plumber's butt to the max. We were all cracking up at that, but J. P. didn't seem to mind.

One of the reasons we were doing this in the frigidness of January rather than in the humidity of July was because the conditions were optimal. That is, the water level was at ten feet (the exact depth of the nets) and its coldness would slow the gars down, making them easier to handle. But since we weren't getting anything in that first hole, we moved on to the mother of all gar holes, where there'd been twelve gars pinging the night before. No doubt, they were still in there—because this was the deepest, darkest hole around, and in the winter, gar just sit there on the bottom, piled up like cordwood.

We put one block net upstream, one block net downstream, and Lindsey anchored the U.S. Fish and Wildlife boat below that. Tommy and J. P. and I were then sent out to spread more nets between the block nets. We did that, then went back to the boat anchored downstream, where they were assembling the shark-cage thing—which was actually a holding pen for gar to revive in after being worked on.

In the meantime, it was warming up, and we all thought it strange that the gar weren't rolling. Of course, they're more lethargic in the winter, but the team had seen them porpoising a month before.

It was coming up on 11:00 a.m., and since no gar had breached yet, Reid decided we should go out there and drag a chain to stir them up. So that's what we did. It was about ten feet long and hung on a rope. We could hear the links clanging against each other under water, but it wasn't enough to rile them up.

After that, we dropped a net in "the honey hole," which is a hole inside the larger hole. And as we began laying the next one, a jug on the honey-hole net started bopping.

"We got one," Tommy said, and we motored on over and he got in the bow and started pulling up the net.

I could see it in there, a thick six-footer, but probably more like seven feet—since gator gar are always larger than you think they are. That's just the way it is: You think one's five feet long, but it's actually six, because gar are deceiving.

Whatever the case, this one was definitely bigger than any of the six-and-a-half-footers I'd caught on the Trinity River, that's for sure, and it was a beauty: all silvery and wide across the back and thrashing in the mesh—which gar can't see because it's black. They swim right into it, get their teeth caught, snag their gills, roll around and get tangled. This one, however, was only caught by a thread.

Tommy and J. P. started working a sling beneath it, but I could tell it wasn't going to work. I suggested getting a line under the pectoral fins like I'm used to doing over in Texas, but they said, "no," and kept trying to maneuver the sling. In less than a minute, it twisted off.

Another jug was bouncing on another net, though, so we went over there and hauled it up. It looked like a five-footer, so it was actually a six-footer. The three of us worked together, got that sling under the fish, and hoisted it into the boat. By the time we got it untangled, then lifted it into the eight-foot tub in the middle of the boat, all of us were slimed with gargoo.

Bringing it back to the U.S. Fish and Wildlife boat, we got it in the sling again, then transferred the fish to Lindsey and Reid to weigh and measure: eighty-six pounds, 174 centimeters. Those are the measurements I recorded, because their tape measure was metric and I chose to record pounds rather than kilos.

We then put this fish in the six-foot tub which had a special-shaped board in it that kept the fish's head under water with its tail in the air. This allowed Reid to move in with a syringe full of green liquid, which he slid beneath a scale and injected into the gar's meat so it would be sedated and easier to deal with. Meanwhile, Richard attached a thin little tag, about three inches long, down toward the base of the tail. Basically, it was a piece of wire coated in orange plastic with numbers on it.

Ed then sterilized a drill bit and bored through the muscle underneath the dorsal fin. He made two holes, stuck two long needles through each one, and because the needles were hollow, he was able to slip two harness wires right through them. When Ed pulled the needles out, the cigar-shaped transmitter was attached and there were two wires going through the fish's back and out the other side. Ed crimped the wires, then rolled the gar onto its belly to take blood samples for DNA.

Tommy and J. P. and I, however, took off to get more gar. The jugs were bouncing around out there, and there were at least two fish in at least two nets. We pulled one up and got a gar the length of the one we just brought in. This one had a deformed head, because somebody probably conked it on the noggin when it was young, or maybe it got run over by a boat. Who knows? We named it Lumphead, then went upstream to the block net.

"You want to pull it up?" Tommy asked, so I said "Sure." And when I did, there was a monster in there. The first thing I saw was its tail, which was one of the hugest I'd ever seen, all black-spotted and tinged red. This fish was only snagged in the head, so suddenly it was an urgent situation.

Tommy dropped to the deck and tried to shove the gar more into the net as J. P. came up with the sling. We all tried to get it under its belly, but it kept swinging into open water.

This was no time to screw around. I jumped up and grabbed a rope. I was going to get a length around its girth then haul it out Texas-style. But by the time I dropped back to the deck, that gar was swimming upstream and Tommy and J. P. were cursing it.

Firing up the engine, though, we shot upstream and laid another block net. Tommy was saying it weighed 150 and J. P. was saying 170. To me it looked like a six-and-a-half-footer, so it must've been a foot longer.

Taking Lumphead back to the other boat, I couldn't help noticing how J. P. and Tommy kept calling it "him," when it's common knowledge that the big ones are always female. Or, at least, that's what Captain Kirk told me, so that's what I'd always repeated, and had even published a couple of times.

"You guys keep calling her a him," I put in. "But aren't all gator gars over thirty pounds female?"

"Naww," Tommy said, laughing at that. "That's a bunch of b.s."

Then he explained how a hatchery manager named Ricky Campbell in Tupelo had just given a presentation debunking that myth. Something about a 150-pound male with over ten pounds of gonads in it—

And this, of course, rocked my gar world. Not that it's a big deal, but now I didn't know who to believe. Or what to believe. Or if I should ever be so quick to believe something so simple again when it can be turned so easily on its head.

Anyway, we shot back to the U.S. Fish & Wildlife boat where the previous gar was recovering in the holding pen. Then hoisting Lumphead in the sling, we weighed him in (yes, *him*—for the sake of convenience) at ninety pounds. And 179 centimeters. Meaning six-foot-something.

All afternoon, we kept going out and pulling up nets, catching six-foot gator gar. They were pretty much all the same size, so therefore from the same generation. Or as J. P. put it, they were "litter mates."

And as the sun came out, and as the junky motor kept breaking down (prompting J. P. to rig up a rip cord with a rope while Tommy conked its gears with a weight), it warmed up to fifty-something degrees—enough to shed my mucousy sweater and wrestle gar in my T-shirt.

We caught one that weighed 108 pounds (184 centimeters) and then one that weighed 115. None of them had ever been tagged, so technically, the population was going up, according to the elusive equation.

But then we snagged another six-footer, rolling in the shallow end. It didn't look very good when we pulled it up. There were these goobery gobs hanging all over it, all greenish and brownish and stringy with yellow streaks. This gar had a transmitter on it and a metal tag on its tail that had rubbed the skin raw on the back fin. It was a bloody mess, and when we brought it back to Reid, neither he nor Lindsey could identify that fungusy stuff. Samples were taken and put in a jar.

We went out again, got one that weighed 102. Then we caught another one—same size, same weight—with a transmitter on it. This one was also covered in those fuzzy-looking loogies. More samples were collected.

Following this, we saw a tailfin sticking up in the net sunk in the honey hole. It was completely still, but we went over there and hauled it up. It was the littlest sucker of the day, looking like four feet long, so no doubt a five-footer. And like the big one that got away, it was only snagged by the head and working its way out of the net. Then it was taking off.

Tommy, however, shot his arm into the water, grabbed its head, and flung the whole fish into the net. Its teeth got tangled in the mesh, so we just hauled the net up on the bow and the fish came with it. This one weighed seventy-five. We named it Junior, and took it back to the anchored boat.

Then we had some untangling to do. About forty-five minutes ago, we'd seen a float bouncing on a net and had tried to haul it up, but it was hung up on a log. When another float started doinking, we'd abandoned it and gone for the other gar, hoping the fish on the stuck net would free itself. Otherwise, it could drown.

So we went back to that snagged net and Tommy and I tried to yank it up. It refused to give, even when J. P. threw it in reverse and tried to tow it out, almost yanking us into the drink.

It was a losing battle. We were pulling and straining and the net wasn't giving an inch. I'd already settled on giving up, but Tommy kept on pulling and J. P. kept throttling back. Then I felt something snap. Then something else. It was coming free.

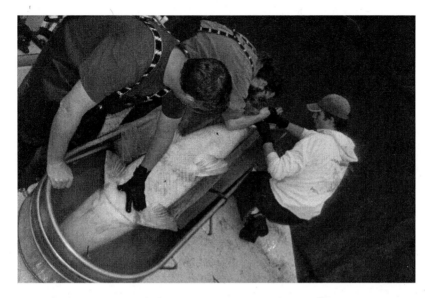

Reid Adams, Ed Kluender and Richard Walker attach a transmitter to a seven-foot-one Arkansas alligator gar. Photo by Mark Spitzer.

"There's something in it," Tommy said. "I can feel its weight."

And when it came up, it was a long white belly, at least six feet long. And when we got it to the surface, it was the biggest fattest alligator gar of the whole day, still alive and twisting in the mesh. It took three of us to get it in the boat.

That one weighed 168 and was 213 centimeters long. And since J. P. noted that 210 centimeters equals seven feet, this fish was an inch longer.

By late afternoon it was overcast and getting colder. People were starting to put on coats and the sun was going down when Tommy got a call on his cell phone.

"We need you to aerate a gar," Reid told him, downstream around the bend.

We went on back. It was Junior, floating belly up in the holding pen.

"He's full of air," Reid said.

We got Junior in a sling parallel to the running boat and motored slowly downstream. I was holding the sling and Tommy had two bare arms in the freezing water and was holding Junior's head up. This is how you revive a gar.

But every time we stopped to let it swim off, it would take a few strokes then roll belly up. Because Junior was refusing to burp. Or couldn't burp. So all that air in its gut was killing it.

I got an arm under Junior's belly, though, and as we motored along with its mouth wide open (which is always an encouraging sign) I massaged its stomach, right where that bubble of air was.

Or gas, I thought, reflecting on E. L. Mark's *Lepidosteus* study from 1890. He was a Cambridge professor who'd gone down to Black Lake in New York, where he got some "gar-pike" spawn, which he brought back on the train in a bucket. Mark raised these young-of-year in the lab, with the objective of figuring out why they rise to the surface, gulp air, then sink and release bubbles. All sorts of data on gar burps and gar farts was compiled. Hundreds of pages, hundreds of hours. Special tanks with funnels and tubes to collect gar gasses were used for analysis. The conclusion being . . . gars release oxygen, nitrogen and carbon dioxide.

But not Junior, who refused to stay upright. So in the end, we had to hand Junior off to Richard and Reid and Lindsey and Ed, then get out there to collect the nets, which were full of sticks and leaves and trash. By the time we got them all hauled in, my back was sore, the sun had set, and Junior was still swimming phlegmatically on his back.

We motored upriver in the dark, following the Fish and Wildlife boat—to a sandbar where we all got out and stood around waiting for Junior to burp. He had enough strength left in his pectoral fins to keep himself balanced in a foot of water, but every time he pushed off, he went belly up, so then we'd have to bring him back and set him up again.

"If we had a tube," Lindsey said, "we could blow some bubbles down there and maybe he'd burp."

Lindsey then explained to me how last time they were out here they had a bunch of gar in a tub and every time one burped, the others would follow suit.

Meanwhile, Ed was unscrewing the top of a float and lowering it under water, right next to Junior. Ed then tipped the jug and a bunch of bubbles broke from it. He did this a few times, and after a bit, Junior answered, releasing a few bubbles of his own. This went on for twenty minutes, Junior sometimes squeezing out three or four little bubbles, but not enough to shake it off and swim free.

So we all kept standing there, shivering and slimed and waiting to catch pneumonia. It was nine at night now, we'd been at it for more than fourteen hours, and we were jonesing to get home to our girlfriends and wives. Or, in the case of J. P., "a twelve-pack of Miller Lite, not none of that Sam Adam's crap!"

Junior belched a good one once, and we cheered, but after that it was no-go. Maybe it was the fact that we were all standing there, shining lights down on him. Or maybe it was something else.

I asked Reid where all that air in Junior had come from.

"It just happens sometimes," he replied. Meaning some gar go through the surgery no problem, but others don't always fare so well. Basically, the longer you have them out of the water, the more stressed they get. And the more they get stressed, the redder their fins get. A year or so ago, they'd lost a big one. It was a 180-pounder, I believe, that got so traumatized from getting turned over and moved from tub to tub that it just up and died. This also happened back in 2000 with a 154-pounder noted in an Arkansas-based study by William Layher. That fish "succumbed to stress."

Gar may look tough, but they're as fragile as the ecosystem. And in this narration, they're a metaphor for it.

Anyhow, we were all worn out and freezing, but none of us could leave Junior's side. It was almost ridiculous. I mean, here we were, seven men, waiting around for a gar to burp, so we could go home and eat some cow, or chicken, or pig—when the kind of fish we were waiting for, in a sense, had never been given such consideration in the past. Back in the day, someone would just smack it over the head with a paddle and leave it on the shore for the vultures.

Now, however, things were different. Every alligator gar counted. Every one was valuable and could vanish just like that, taking its contribution to the gene pool with it.

And since no one had ever seen or caught a juvenile alligator gar in these waters more than just a few inches long, and since most of these gar were Junior's size or larger, it stood to reason that Junior was the runt of the only successful spawn in decades. We're still trying to get a handle on gar aging. The point being: For all the seasons they've been spawning in this river, the conditions (hydrology, temperature, vegetation) hadn't been conducive for propagation since Junior's litter. And since there was no telling when or if another spawn would ever take, it was important for us to stick around and help a gar out.

But we couldn't stay there all night long, so Ed suggested that we take off the transmitter and leave Junior in the shallow water. That way, if Junior croaked, the equipment could be used again. If, however, Junior made it, he'd be tagged and accounted for and maybe we'd even catch him again.

So we left him there to live or die, and none of us felt very good about that.

The running boat was out of gas, so the U.S. Fish and Wildlife boat was towing us upstream through a labyrinth of stumps and logs. I was discussing Junior's chances for survival with Tommy, who basically shrugged and invoked the old adage "out of sight, out of mind."

Which got me to thinking about all the fish in my life that were out there now, swimming around with lures in their jaws, or wound around some log, or searching for prey with only one eye. I had injured hundreds of fish, rubbed off their protective slime, ripped up their throats, and thrown countless creatures back to die.

And now here I was on my own virtual Trinity River, with scores of big gar under me, around me, in my vicinity. Gar, I was thinking earlier, that I might go for—because that's my connection with fish. That's why I fish. To get them! Which is why I want to keep them alive and keep them around. So I can hook them. Play them. Admire and release them.

But now I wasn't so sure that I could come out here and cast a grass carp into that hole. Because what if a gar swallowed the hook and I ripped up its stomach lining? What if it got infected, or covered in that snotty sludge? Or what if one got wound around a sunken log and I couldn't get it up, like that seven-footer Tommy and I almost never recovered? It would be too easy to hurt these gar—who are essentially now *my gar*.

So the question became, W*ould I become like J. P., a reformed hunter of the big ones?* And the question following this was, *Do I even have what it takes to restrain myself from fishing for them?* Man, I was confused—and still am. I mean . . . the whole male/female thing. . . . the casualties in the name of Science . . . the crazy continuum of all those fish I cannot see, swimming around messed up from me . . . it was almost enough to make me give up gator gar-fishing forever.

And an hour later, driving back in the truck, I could see that Ed was feeling pretty much the same way. He was sullen and somber in the back seat, and when Reid asked him why he was so quiet, Ed told us he was wondering if we should've stayed longer with Junior.

We changed that conversation, though, to Lindsey and Ed's upcoming trip to Texas. Basically, it was a code-red situation over there. The state had begun counting gator gar, and Captain Kirk was in on it, tagging the ones his clients caught. Still, they couldn't tag enough fast enough, and every day the population was going down—thanks to next to no restrictions on bowfishing, commercial fishing, and out-of-state trophy hunting.

So they were bringing in Tommy and Lindsey to net and tag and attach transmitters, so that Texas can do what Arkansas is doing: gathering data to put to use, to protect the big ones and bring their numbers up to snuff. Because, as Tommy noted in his thesis proposal, there's "a 125% increase in the number of jeopardized fishes (i.e., extinct, endangered, or vulnerable status) from the previous 20 years."

This, of course, was something we were all aware of, especially in this new era of global warming, when we try solve problems after years of being warned that we've already caused irreparable damage. But at least we're focusing more on the loss of our resources now, which is encouraging for gator gar and everything else, but maybe not enough to prevent the extinction of the most fascinating fish there is.

Hopefully, though, the population of gar-huggers will increase with the spring floods. Because at this point, vain as this may sound, nature needs more of us for more of them. Because if we don't document the fact that they're going down, and if we don't protect them from thrill-seeking fishermen like me and bloodthirsty bowhunters like J. P. (who can barely curb the urge to conquer what they love), and if we can't provide gator gar access to the right vegetation in properly flooded spawning grounds, we'll be saying sayonara to a species that's been here since the Jurassic. And if they go, signaling the disintegration of yet another link in a steadily collapsing chain, I tell you what: We'll be out of sight and out of mind sooner than later, and gone with the Arkansas alligator gar.

13

A Psychological History of the Arkansas Alligator Gar with Recommendations for Its Future

A Polemic

BACK BEFORE THE Choctaw and Cherokee and Chickasaw and Seminole and Creek and Spanish and French, back before the saber-toothed cat roamed the Ozarks along with the woodland buffalo, back before the ivory-bills were plentiful throughout the Delta, before the mammoths and mastodons ranged through the prairies and swamps, when the brunt of what is now Arkansas had yet to be deforested—way way back before that, in the Mesozoic and Paleozoic eras of the continent, in the rivers and marshes and bayous and vast sprawling flood plains that provided ideal spawning grounds for prehistoric monster fish sometimes surpassing twelve feet in length—back then, alligator gar ruled.

And for the next 300 million years, this practically non-evolving species continued to endure. As Jay Drott put it in an article titled "Timeless Prowler," gator gar survived "millions of years of geological and evolutionary chaos."[1] In fact, gar survived three or four ice ages, dinosaurs, the Quapaw and Caddo and Osage nations, the settling of North America, and all the agriculture and industry that came with that—to become one of the oldest living fish families on the planet.

But then, after eons of being the apex freshwater predator in North America, something happened in the twentieth century. Basically, alligator gar numbers across the country went from hundreds of thousands (if not millions) down to the thousands, and, in the state of Arkansas, to less than a few hundred. And like all plummeting populations of twenty-first-century threatened species, this collapse was due to the actions of a more recent species—one that hasn't even been around for a mere million

117

years. One whose nature is to impact nature with a devastating and oftentimes irreversible force—which is why all alligator gar populations are now facing the prospect of a complete collapse.

As Lee Holt, a fisheries biologist and member of the Alligator Gar Management Plan team with the Arkansas Game & Fish Commission, stated, "There's no doubt that if we don't step up right now . . . it's imminent. I mean, this crash you're talking about, if we don't do something, it's going to happen. There's no doubt in my mind, because the numbers just aren't there."[2]

And Holt knows, since he co-authored the study "Alligator Gar (*Atractosteus spatula*) Life History and Habitat Use in the Cache, Mississippi and White Rivers" with U.S. Fish and Wildlife Service hatcheries manager Ricky Campbell. In 2007, Holt received a wildlife grant from the U.S. Fish and Wildlife Service (with matching funds from Arkansas Game & Fish) for research and equipment involved in the sampling and monitoring of Arkansas alligator gar.

Because of the dangerously low numbers of this fish, though, Holt has been able to document only a few specimens in the river systems of his study. Fortunately, though, two breeding populations have recently been identified in the Ouachita and Fourche LaFave rivers, and with assistance from biologists and researchers, data is now being gathered to help protect these gator gar. Meaning the imminent crash Holt warns us of can be avoided if we take the necessary steps. At this time (spring 2009), however, the eradication of the northern snakehead in Lee County's Piney Creek has taken priority over efforts to conserve alligator gar.

But before we get into what's being done and not being done and what can be done, here's a simple overview of the dynamics that almost wiped out the hugest, most primordial fish in the alluvial state of Arkansas.

Not much is known about the relationship between Native Americans and alligator gar, but we can speculate that it was one based on utility and respect. Utility because it's well known that many tribes constructed arrowheads from gar scales, and respect because there are still different types of "garfish dances" performed to this day by Creek and Chickasaw tribes. Many of these dances are fertility rites that pay homage to gar, whereas other dances employ garfish teeth in "purification ritual[s] connected with the summer ceremonies."[3]

Also, Native American axes with effigies of garfish carved on them were discovered along the Arkansas River near Fort Smith. According to the Spiro Mounds artifact database, "The distal end [of one axe] has a carving thought to be a garfish head. It consists of a large mouth full of teeth and a round eye at the blade."[4] This information provides further evidence of the significant cultural role gar played in the lives of the ancient people of the region.

But then came the Europeans. And in settling the continent, they sought to drive all "savage" elements as far away as possible from their communities—especially during Thomas Jefferson's presidency, when an aggressive campaign to clear millions of Native Americans from half of the country followed the Louisiana Purchase. With a few exceptions, the indigenous people were massacred en masse, forced into the swamps and deserts, made to walk the Trail of Tears, and isolated in concentration camps which evolved into reservations, because they threatened the life-styles envisioned by the colonizing cultures. And since the alligator gar, with its ferocious jaws and serpentine girth, represented a type of pagan wildness similar to that of the Indians, this truly native American species was feared and dispossessed of its habitat as well.

Generally speaking, from the moment the French discovered alligator gar on this continent (Samuel de Champlain representing, 1609), this eight- to ten-foot American fish with its upper, double row of very sharp teeth was demonized as not only having the supernatural snout of a hog, but as being a brutal mutant that "makes war on all the other fish."[5] Subsequently, this species was condemned in the New World for being an aggressive freak of nature, based solely on its fierce appearance. Driven by a distaste for this creature and an ignorance of the bio-diversity necessary to sustain healthy environments, it only took a few hundred years of oral history to manifest the gar's reputation into being "unquestionably the most soundly hated fresh water fish in the state."[6]

And with rhymesters like Phil Carspecken capitalizing on poetry that claims "the Devil, with the sole intent to mar/Produced that foul abor-tion that we call the Billy Gar,"[7] it didn't take much to influence the old-school church folk in this country that gar were out of the graces of God —especially when words like "abortion" were employed. At this point, however (the 1920s), gar had already been labeled with common names like "devil fish" and derivatives thereof.

The unknown author of an 1853 article called "Fishing at the West" once aligned "this savage fish" with "the leviathan of Scripture," asking, "Canst thou draw out leviathan with a hook? or his tongue with a cord which thou lettest down? canst thou fill his skin with barbed irons? or his head with fish-spear?"[8] Regardless of the answer, it was obvious by the mid-nineteenth century where gar stood in the standing of the church. With that "baneful gleam of their eye" and "their wicked jaws"[9] characterizing the species into the twentieth century, and with a highly Pentecostal obsession with serpents and talking snakes throughout the Baptist South, the vilified gar began to represent a kind of demonic missing link—but, ironically, not to the Arctic fishapod *Tiktaalik roseae*, which evolved from a type of gar into a type of alligator 375 million years ago. Nope, to the extremely fundamental demographics of Arkansas, the gar was considered a cast-out hybrid Devil spawn—like a sea monster, or a human-hating lizard-monster fused from the body parts of reptiles, birds of prey, and whatever other monstrosities existed in the superstitions of the people.

Historically, and in almost all cultures, such terrifying crossbreeds are considered "dragons"—an identity gator gar became associated with in the 1800s. Since Arkansas has always had a colorful history of storytelling (particularly in nineteenth-century newspaper stories that embellished the idea of regional monsters), this identity stuck for decades. Consequently, quite a few ichthyological commentators like George Powers Dunbar hopped on the dragon bandwagon, dramatizing the gator gar as a "river robber [that] rolls his huge form through the deep river . . . his capacious and horrid jaws wide open and his sinewy tail dealing death on every side."[10] Until eventually, as Charlie Burton noted in a 1970 issue of *Arkansas Game & Fish Magazine*, "Destroying a gar [became] comparable to slaying a dragon that was wreaking havoc on the countryside, devouring women and children."[11]

Burton also remarked that "the gar's physical appearance caused this typecasting."[12] A typecasting, of course, that came stock with other inhuman, and even anti-human, qualities. For example, an article called "Capturing the Marauding Arkansas Gar," published in a 1941 issue of *Spot Magazine*, pigeonholed alligator gar as "ugly, mean" and "loathsome."[13] This typecasting of the gar's temperament was then embraced by a slew of writers, and a barrage of unchecked stereotyping took off like wildfire. Take Johnnie M. Gray's statement in 1966, for example, when he called "The alligator gar pike (Pepisoseus spatula)" [*sic*] "a fierce and greedy fresh water predator,"[14] or the notes compiled by Carol Griffee for *Arkansas Wildlife: A History* (1998), which also reflect a name-calling mentality: "The alligator gar is so ugly that it's questionable whether it's loved even by its mother."[15] Add to this the personification of gars having "flat eyes rimmed with hate"[16] in a 1961 issue of *Southern Angler's Guide* with Joel M. Vance's

1984 depiction of the "baleful, impersonal lack of compassion in its eyes,"[17] and what you've got is not just a seething and vengeful bastard fish, but a psychopathic one at that. In fact, such speculation on the intentions of the alligator gar led to its portrayal as a piscine terrorist as early as the 1850s, when it was tagged as "the terror and abhorrence of the boatmen on" the Mississippi.[18] Hence the expression, "'as mean as Gar broth,' being the example of all that is vile."[19]

It's obvious that a lot of judgment has been cast on alligator gar. Judgment that's typified best by the hypocrisy of gar haters like Col. J. G. Burr of Texas, who was the Director of Research and Public Relations for the Texas Game, Fish and Oyster Commission back in the 1930s. Burr was the inventor of the *Electrical Gar Destroyer*, a small boat that barged through the bayous zapping thousands of gars to death, and killing at least a hundred times more turtles in the process.[20] Under the false impression that the alligator gar "attains a length of 20 feet or more," "is very destructive to all sorts of fishes," and the "flesh is worthless,"[21] this quizzical conservationist was also prone to making contradictory statements about the value of wildlife. For instance, in a pamphlet titled *Conservation of Wildlife Resources*, Burr wrote that "nature should be wisely used and not wasted," then later quipped, "Who could blame the boys or any one else for shooting them? Sparrows, blackbirds and crows may be shot at sight."[22] When discussing gar, Burr was also partial to making opinionated statements that classified bass and crappie as "good fish,"[23] thereby implying that gar are *bad*. But as Aldo Leopold once put it, "there is no such thing as a good or a bad species; a species may get out of hand, but to terminate its membership in the land by human fiat is the last word in anthropomorphic arrogance."[24]

Anyway, with anthropomorphically arrogant neighbors like the colonel mowing their lawns in such a careless manner, it's reasonable to conclude that Arkansas didn't feel it was necessary to maintain its own yard any better—or with any more respect for the value of native species. As a result, gar were "considered an obnoxious fish" in their "Relation to Man"[25] throughout the state. The "superabundance of these [species] and of other such trash,"[26] as envisioned in the eyes of the gar-loathing masses, then fed a general garanoia that characterized "throwbacks like the gar [as] a menace to modern animal life [which] . . . will wreak vast destruction unless they themselves are destroyed by game lovers and sportsmen."[27]

This latter statement, being characteristic of the propaganda of the times (especially in Germany), was published in the 1941 issue of *Spot Magazine* mentioned earlier—a publication that had no qualms whatsoever about reinforcing the misinformation that the alligator gar "is so voracious it eats its own weight every 36 hours."[28] Of course, it's never been a secret that there's no means to an end more effective for ridding an area of a population than combining a distaste for its gene pool with a vigorous campaign to disseminate destructive misinformation. Thus, the editors of *Spot* and other magazines with anti-gator gar agendas knew exactly what they were doing.

I could go further into the connections between the shockingly similar twentieth-century campaigns to exterminate various detested populations in Europe and America, but I'll suffice it to say that when it came to the dynamics of ghettoization, Nazi rhetoric provided an influential model for various voices of "pamphlet lit" in the United States. When calling upon fisherman to destroy gar without hesitation, based on the disinformation that this "threat" to our natural resources held no value whatsoever,[29] it goes without question that state agencies employed the same type of fear-mongering language made popular in Europe between world wars.

As Arkansas wildlife writer Keith "Catfish" Sutton points out, for "more than 200 years, [alligator gar] have been persecuted due to the mistaken notion that they harm gamefish populations."[30] Basically, this persecution was allowed to go uncontested, because an ignorant and unfavorable attitude toward gar manifested itself into a mob mentality at a time when racial and class tensions in an economically stressed America created an atmosphere conducive to scapegoating. This blame game (mostly visible in attacks upon Communists) was allowed to mushroom because gar just didn't live up to the popular construct of fish-beauty as exemplified in bass and trout. Additionally, being judged guilty through association with dragons and snakes and devils and the like encouraged rumors that portrayed gar as disposable chimeras worthy of our most-profound hatreds. Just take a look at the titles of the articles listed in the endnotes here (with key words like "monster," "prowler," "marauding," etc.) and it's clear that the pre-Cold War media in the United States sacrificed objectivity for marketing considerations.

But there was another element at work, which contributed to the virtual blacklisting of gator gar in a country historically founded on its connection with the wild. This connection, however, which was embraced in the 1800s by the Transcendentalists (who strove to establish a national identity based on a body of literature that celebrated an untamed landscape), lost its focus as the nation strove for modernization. In this process, the innocence of our pristine wilderness was compromised as the land was

Two men and a 210-pound, eight-foot-two-inch gator gar lynched in Hempstead County, Arkansas, in 1921. Photo courtesy of Keith Sutton.

razed for agriculture and urbanization. Coal and oil began being prized over vast expanses of nature, and as a result, an unchecked petrochemical industry merged with the war machine to develop extremely damaging insecticides and gasses for mass murdering, which took priority over public health and safety. Like tens of thousands of other species, the gator gar became a casualty in this shift in priorities.

An argument can also be made that the atomic bomb was developed and implemented to make things easier for Americans, with little forethought of the consequences for the rest of the world. Hence, this dark side of "the American Dream" had its effect on foreign as well as domestic policy, which led to gar suffering along with eagles, ospreys, bobcats, manatees, and tens of thousands of other species. As Alfred C. Weed, assistant curator of fishes at the Field Museum of Natural History in Chicago, observed in 1923, "Man is so constituted that he considers the value of other living things solely on a basis of his own comfort or convenience. A fish is useful or valuable to him only as he can see some direct relation to his needs or pleasures. On this basis, much has been said against the gars and very little in their favor."[31] In sum, an illiterate oral tradition on this continent (and when I write "illiterate," I literally mean *unread,* as in *literally uninformed by life science studies*) led to an apocryphal revisionist history regarding gar that lasted for almost four centuries.

In the late-twentieth century, though, scientists began to seriously question what was going on with this species. Discoveries were made and data was collected, with fishery-management specialists like Dennis L. Scarnecchia concluding that gar need strategic management plans because they've been "misunderstood."[32] This misunderstanding, or ignorance—also evident in our attitude toward wolves, bears, panthers, and other creatures that rarely ever attack humans—is partially responsible for the highly precarious situation we are now facing when it comes to reclaiming extirpated species. Still, despite all the advances in our knowledge of gator gar and their role in the environment, we lack a major understanding of this fish, especially when it comes to what can be done to repair what we've screwed up.

As Robin Huggins stated in a 1992 article published in *Arkansas Wildlife* magazine, "Today, little is known about the status of alligator gar's population in Arkansas."[33] Seventeen years later, this is still the case—which is why it's high time to cast off the baggage of perpetrating falsehoods based on myopic aesthetics that don't do anyone any good. Because ultimately, alligator gar aren't just an endangered species that doesn't merit enough public sympathy to be federally protected, they're also representative of all the fragile components in our ecosystem that we are presently frittering away based on our faith in what is *good* and what is *bad,* rather than what we've proven to be true through objective study. So in this time of global warming and the mass collapse of species worldwide, it would be wise to identify the real dangers in our midst, in order to sustain for as long as possible everything else we don't understand. Because like it or not, this planet is a single body on the decline, whose health and future depends upon the effective functioning of an extremely complex network of organisms, all of them co-dependent on each other.

As Sutton phrased it in his 1998 *In-Fisherman* article "Gar Wars," one "of the most fantastic sport-fisheries in the world was born and died in Arkansas in less than two decades."[34] This sport-fishery was a tourism industry of rod-and-reel fishing for alligator gar, and the decades referred to are the 1940s and '50s. Back then, various publications touted the state as a gator gar mecca, where anglers from around the world could use deep-sea tackle to catch furious, leaping goliath-fish weighing well over a hundred pounds. Such publicity was effective, especially on the lower White, Cache, Mississippi, Arkansas, Red, L'Anguille, Ouachita and St. Francis rivers, where word-of-mouth as well as newspaper and magazine articles brought steady business to local guides.

Most of these alligator gar were caught on piano wires and finished off with bullets, shotgun slugs, and arrows through the skull. The big ones were plentiful for a while, and landing seven-footers was much more common than it is today. The following information, collected by E. W. Gudger, honorary associate in ichthyology at the American Museum of Natural History, provides a typical sampling of some of the larger gator gar caught in the state during the early '40s:

> From Arkansas, I have the following authentic records. The late Louis Reitzammer, my most valuable correspondent, at Arkansas City on the Mississippi River, sent me these: (1) 7 feet 4 inches long, 43 inches in girth,* 154 pounds on the scales; (2) 7 feet 5 inches long, 49 inches in girth,* 163 pounds weight; (3) 7 feet 6 inches long, 32 inches in girth, 186 pounds weight.† Then he added, "You need not be surprised at accounts of 10-footers. I am satisfied that we have them here that large, but we have not been successful in landing them." . . . My former student, the late Dr. Henry Thibault, caught two big fellows near his home. Here are his

figures: (1) 7 feet 8 inches long, 178 pounds in weight; (2) 9 feet 2 inches long, 232 pounds in weight. This latter is next to the largest fish of which I have been able to get an authentic record. It can be relied on, for the man who made it was one of the most meticulous persons I ever knew. He wrote me that the head alone measured 2 feet long. And in the same locality, my friend J.R. Alexander measured a head that was 12 inches wide between the eyes.[35]

Seven-footers, of course, are still occasionally caught in Arkansas (I recently helped pull in a seven-foot-one 168-pounder), but back in the 1950s, thousands were hauled in, shot, and discarded. As Arkansas gator gar guide John Fox recalled: "By [1962] . . . alligator gar were gone from the L'Anguille and St. Francis rivers. . . . In 1954, 1955, 1956, and 1957, people were coming in from all over the country. . . . The fishing began petering out in 1957 or 1958, and I just didn't feel right taking people out any more . . . by 1959 . . . we had cleaned out the rivers."[36]

Fox, who used to "catch 12 or more a day over 100 pounds,"[37] also noted, "We thought we were doing right getting rid of them, only to find out later that we killed the goose that laid the golden egg."[38] This sentiment was shared by gar guide John Heuston of Little Rock, who noted that in the late '50s "the general opinion was that these were predators on gamefish . . . They would pile the gars up that they caught on the gravel bars and pour gasoline on them and set fire to them. Maybe 100 of them at a time. They caught tremendous numbers of these big gars, and slowly the fishery began to decline."[39] These figures agree with the observations of W. M. (Bill) Apple, a columnist for the Arkansas Wildlife Federation, who wrote, "In one 12-mile stretch [on the lower White River] 600 gar weighing over 100 pounds were taken in one summer season."[40] By the time the 1990s rolled around, the behemoths were rarely caught in the state. In 1997, professional fishing guide Charley Alter was asked if there were any big gar left in the rivers, and he replied with a flat-out "No."[41]

Fishing the alligator gar out of Arkansas rivers, however, was only a single factor in a series of events that ate into the species' capacity to reproduce. As gar specialist Dr. Allyse Ferrara of Nicholls State University explains in her dissertation on the life history of alligator gar, "Long-lived aquatic organisms with low fecundity or variable or infrequent recruitment . . . are highly susceptible to population decline due to anthropogenic factors (i.e., overfishing, habitat loss and alteration)."[42] Consequently, when excessive rod-and-reel fishing for gator gar was replaced by bowhunting, the number of gar "that weighed 140 and 150 pounds . . . [and] were 50 and 60 and 70 years old"[43] plummeted severely.

Without question, "sportsman-physician and president of the Arkansas Wild Life Federation" Dr. Sherrod Drennen of Stuttgart made a heavy impact on the state's supply of alligator gar. He teamed up with archer L. E. Piper and together they became the pre-World War II poster boys for hauling in mammoth gator gars then rapidly dispatching of them. The previously mentioned issue of *Spot Magazine* depicted Drennen as the leader in a "crusade to eliminate [alligator gar] from the river."[44] Drennen's justification for wiping out hundreds of gator gar, according to his grandson Larry Drennen Bouchard, was that "gar were daily consuming their weight in other game fish . . . from his perspective, they were nuisance fish."[45]

As it's already been established, an unfavorable attitude toward gar influenced the widespread dissemination of misleading information, which led to a species-specific *genocide*—since that's the term that's applied when attempts are made to eliminate a gene pool. So regardless of whether

Cache River Alligator Gar, Arkansas. The archer is L. E. Piper and the man in the hat is Dr. Sherrod Drennen. The photo was taken sometime in the late 1930s or early 1940s. Lew Piper, L. E. Piper's son, claims the picture was taken by a photographer from St. Louis, but Steve Wright, author of *Arkansas Duck Hunter's Almanac*, credits Edgar Queeny.

Drennen and others involved in this jihad on gator gar saw themselves as saviors of sacred populations, or whether they just wanted a righteous excuse to shoot 'em up for fun, the bottom line is that they sanctioned their own behavior as morally appropriate and socially condoned.

Such was the case with Arkansas archer William McCreary and various other bowhunters hungry for the blood of gar—but not their meat. According to Mack Roy of Crawfordsville, whose uncle hunted alligator gar back in the '50s, "It never occurred to them to try to eat one, or do anything with it."[46]

But back to Piper, who pioneered bowhunting for gator gar, and not just in Arkansas. The method was effective, and unlike rod-and-reel fishing, once that arrow entered the skull of an alligator gar, there was no potential for catch-and-release. Essentially, Piper popularized a new old sport in the South, which spread to Texas and neighboring states. A "sport" which achieved the outcome Drennen was shooting for, since it surpassed the results of angling, made archery a fashionable method for gator gar trophy hunting, and led to the killing of thousands of jumbo gar throughout their ever-decreasing range.

There are no exact numbers, but what is known is that up until the 1990s there was hardly any regulation in this country on taking alligator gar. As William Layher points out in his 2008 study on the life history of gator gar in the Ouachita River, "Most gar harvest is from commercial fishermen and bow fishing."[47] Hence, in Arkansas (where close to nobody angles for this fish anymore), there are now less than two hundred known alligator gar.[48] Human predators, however, continue to bowhunt gator gar in the state, and destroy them on a regular basis, even though the population is officially "in peril."[49]

So that's where we are today: in the midst of a crashing economy that went belly up because it refused regulation. And the same could happen to the alligator gar, since we are currently dealing with the consequences of not examining the long-term effects of taking the big ones out of our systems. As Layher indicates, since the "biggest number of eggs are laid by the biggest individuals, and the biggest individuals tend to be weeded out of the population . . . the majority of their reproductive potential" vanishes along with them.[50] This is exactly what happened to gator gar in Arkansas, where Fox stated with regret, "If I had them back now, I'd release every one of them."[51]

But it wasn't just over-harvesting and exploitation that led to a phenomenal drop in the Arkansas gator gar population. As countless authorities note, "Their habitat has been destroyed by river channelization and dam construction."[51] This fact is echoed by Ferrara, who refers to Robison and Buchanan, Simon and Wallus, Etnier and Starnes, Metee, et al., and C. Knight in order to affirm that "Reasons for range contraction and population declines of alligator gar are . . . functions of . . . habitat loss and alteration."[52] Citing Welcomme, Jackson, et al., Rasmussen, and Ward and Stanford, Ferrara explains, "The historical range of alligator gar has experienced dramatic flow and habitat alterations due to navigational, flood control, agricultural, and power generation interests (i.e., locks, dams, levees, channel straightening, and dredging) that have reduced the historical connection of floodplains to the main river channel."[53] Of course, a lot of the "habitat degradation . . . [that] made gator gar rare in many waters where they once were abundant,"[54] coincided with the federal works projects of the 1930s, when campaigns to exterminate alligator gar were in full swing across the South.

Whether this be coincidence or a calculated move on the part of assorted corps of engineers, the result—in conjunction with the increasing alligator gar sportfishing/bowhunting industries—was devastating to the species as a whole. In Arkansas, according to Huggins, biologists believed "the once common fish was quickly decimated. . . . partly due to damming and channelization of the White River." Such "detrimental effect[s] on traditional spawning areas"[55] were also noted by stream fisheries management biologist Jeff Quinn, who formed an alligator gar task force in the state in 1999. Though this task force eventually disintegrated, Quinn collected notes explaining how "Montgomery Point Lock and Dam could prevent migration from the White to Mississippi River," how river channel morphology changes "in the White River from Bull Shoals, Norfork, and Greers Ferry Dams" were causing complications, and how "the Arkansas River Navigation Dams block migration."[56] As Layher points out, "you have dike systems that prevent over-flooding and so you no longer have that connectivity, plus the backwaters don't get flooded . . . Consequently, the dams have really hurt the recruitment of [alligator gar] from a reproductive standpoint."[57] These altered river systems in Arkansas, however, only represent a handful of instances of continental constipation hindering gator gar migration.

But it's not just river channel modification and locks and levees physically preventing gator gar from accessing the specific herbaceous vegetation necessary for reproduction; there's also the fact that cold-water discharges from dams have affected the breeding conditions throughout the continent. It only takes a few degrees in temperature to make gar not want to spawn, and that's what's currently occurring throughout their range. Also, the fact that more dams means less flooding, and the fact that the flooding that does happen is strictly controlled, means there is little consideration for the nine days or so needed for gar eggs attached to vegetation to stay submerged in warm-enough water. Add to this the fact that the newborn require another few weeks of marshy protection to feed on mosquito larvae in order grow to a size that can survive in deeper water, and you have a highly complicated equation which demands a virtual harmonic convergence of optimum water temperature, water levels, and access to the right kind of plant life for a spawn to take.

As gar researcher Ed Kluender at the University of Central Arkansas puts it, it's all about the habitat in "the shallow backwater tributaries that get flooded only around spring or in the summer briefly." Kluender also says that it's "a matter of the availability of this [habitat] which determines" if a system can sustain itself successfully and encourage reproduction.[59] Thus, if it's unlikely that the ideal conditions for spawning can be met, stocking and restocking will not matter. As Layher explains, concerning the idea of introducing hatchery gar: "That's all well and good, but what's the purpose? If you're providing them so people can fish for them, if you can get that many that abundant, I guess that's one thing and maybe one benefit, but if there's no place for them to spawn anyway, then you don't have the habitat or you don't reclaim the habitat . . . the only point in doing that [would be] to put the fish in for the fishermen."[60]

Therefore, a vital step in increasing Arkansas alligator gar reproduction will involve habitat reclamation, but in coordination with special attention to providing favorable water levels and temperatures for the young-of-year juveniles to make it out of the highly sensitive spawning grounds. A comprehensive statewide strategy, of course, will be key in establishing a tactic for propagating the species. Fortunately, as Holt indicates, Arkansas Game & Fish is "in the beginning stages of a management plan for the alligator gar."[61]

As Scarnecchia concludes in his quintessential 1992 study on gar and bowfin management, "In waters inhabited by both holosteans and popular game fishes, more emphasis should be on maintaining diversity and balance . . .

rather than on simply eradicating the less stylish species."[62] This is a direct response to Weed's statement (supplied as an epigraph in Scranecchia's article) about humans judging gar in relation to their own comfort and convenience. Weed wrote that "To find the value of the gars we must look at other points,"[63] which is exactly what Scarnecchia did. By examining the ecological role gar play in their indigenous environments, Scarnecchia made official some complete no-brainers that should've been part of our general consciousness for at least a hundred years of gar-eradicating megalomania. Mainly, "In their native habitats, gars and bowfins can be not only desirable for the diversity they provide, but they . . . also function to stabilize the fish community and to provide additional fishing."[64]

Scarnecchia's insistence that gar should be viewed "not merely as nuisances to be destroyed, but as contributors to ecosystem stability and function, to balance among predators and prey, and to more successful angling in the long term,"[65] however, failed to register on the popular radar of anglers and bowhunters in this country. Scarnecchia's article was published in the bulletin of the American Fisheries Society, not *Field and Stream,* so the audience receiving this information was mostly biologists, rather than the vast mass of self-identified "redneck sportsmen," who will be the first to tell you that they ain't open to entertaining other perspectives when it comes to politics and religion.

Without question, this is a stereotype based on values passed down from father to son. And since everyone knows there's sometimes a bit of truth in stereotypes, and since I'd say there's a lot more truth in the stereotypes of humans than there are in those of gar, I'd also say it's fair to state that our resistance to change is based more on ignorance than denial. Because if the facts are out there, debate can exist. And if debate can exist, the scientific method can be put to the test and play a part in debunking myths. In the meantime, though, there's no disputing the findings of scientists like Scarnecchia and James Nelson Gowanloch of the Louisiana Department of Conservation, whose combined research proves that "Gars play an important role in modifying the character of fish populations."[66]

One of the ways gar can modify the character of fish populations is by helping other fish grow as large as possible. As Scarnecchia explains, gar "have been shown to eat mostly small fish, thereby reducing prey fish numbers but increasing the growth rate of survivors."[67] This is exactly the point of the following excerpt, in which Holt's response to an interview question metamorphoses into a back-and-forth between himself and a hypothetical old-timer fisherman:

> For so long it's been bass bass bass, largemouth largemouth largemouth. I mean, that's not the top predator in the food chain. The alligator gar is . . . the Mac Daddy, so to speak. You ask fishermen, "When was the fishing good? About twenty, thirty years ago?"
> "Yeah yeah yeah."
> "Well, what was the alligator gar population like back then?"
> "Aww, they were everywhere."
> "Hmm, what's fishing like now?"
> "Uh, it stinks."[68]

Holt's point is that the alligator gar numbers have dropped so severely that their lack of contribution to the system has led to an imbalance in local populations of fish species in Arkansas. Or in other words, because "that niche is not there anymore,"[69] there are less big fish in the state.

I should also add that since alligator gar eat longnose gar, there is now more competition between longnose gar and bass for medium-sized minnows than there was fifty years ago. Also, since gar and bass live symbiotically in many ways [see Gregory P. Goff's "Brood Care of Longnose Gar (*Lepisosteus osseus*) by Smallmouth Bass (*Micropterus dolomieui*)]," it would be advantageous for bass anglers to help protect alligator gar, rather than perpetrate the poppycock that they feed on mass bass.

For one thing, gator gar just aren't interested in eating spiny-finned fish when softer minnows are available. I've seen this with my own gars in my own tanks. Plus, various food studies (e.g., Kelshaw Bonham's "Food of Gars in Texas," Edgar P. Seidensticker's "Food Selection of Alligator Gar and Longnose Gar in a Texas Reservoir," and the "Food Habits" summary in Layher's "Literature Survey, Status in States of Historic Occurrence, and Field Investigations into the Life History of Alligator Gar in the Ouachita River, Arkansas") have shown that it is extremely rare when alligator gar do feed on bass. Additionally, as Scarnecchia notes, "every time a legal bass is removed [from a body of water] the gar population is favored."[70] And the same goes for catfish, crappie, and other game fish that garner a lot more respect than gar and Rodney Dangerfield.

Biodiversity aside, however, this apex freshwater predator can serve our needs in other ways, especially in controlling highly destructive nonnative species. As fisheries biologist Christopher Kennedy of the Missouri Department of Conservation explained, since alligator gar are the only freshwater fish capable of consuming Asian carp, gator gar could be used to partially control the mushrooming populations of this invasive species currently threatening the entire ecosystem of the Mississippi and the Great Lakes.[71]

Not only that, but gar are the only fish known to eat the notorious northern snakehead, which has been terrorizing ecosystems across the nation for the last few years. The snakehead first burst onto the American consciousness in Maryland following 9/11 and the anthrax attacks, and is now the target of a massive rotenone kill in Lee County, Arkansas. Although official data has not yet been collected on the effectiveness of employing alligator gar to control this destructive species, there is presently a video posted on YouTube ("alligator gar vs. snakehead"), which clearly shows a gator gar swallowing a snakehead.[72]

But back to Scarnecchia's argument regarding the biodiversity-balancing function gar used to play, and can once again play, in their native waters. This is still the most convincing reason to preserve the species, but not just because gar are threatened; there are other species that depend on gar, and an unfathomable network of species that depend on various links in a highly complex chain. As Weed explained, "This is the case with the Yellow Sand (*Lampsilis anodontoides*) Shell, which Mr. R.L. Barney, Director of the U.S. Bureau of Fisheries Biological Station at Fairport, Iowa, says: 'is without a doubt the most valuable shell of the Mississippi drainage.'"[73] After being fertilized, the eggs of this freshwater clam turn into glochidia, which attach to the gills of gar. Gar then act as carriers for a few weeks, and eventually the glochidium drop off. If, however, gar are forced into unsustainable environments (for themselves and/or their passengers), or if gar are not allowed to act as taxis by picking yellow sand shells up in their natural environments, an essential link in a vital chain can easily disappear along with myriad organisms that require access to this niche.

This news, of course, comes at a time of planetary crisis, when shellfish around the world are experiencing cataclysmic crashes and radical mutations. If such overlooked species do not vanish all together (as they are doing daily), then they're likely to do it gradually, with a series of genetic corruptions (thinning of the shells is common) that weaken the species that feed on them.

But it's not just about the species we are conscious of and what these species can do for us, it's also about the species we don't know of yet, which we nevertheless depend upon. Sure, alligator gar (or millions of other interconnected life forms) could be our link to a cure for cancer, or perhaps gar research could show us how to survive the next ice age, but that's not why I've made it my mission to promote the survival of this species.

For me, it's more than the possibility of my float suddenly heading downstream, the action-packed chase that ensues, the explosion on top of the water, the forty-five minutes of horsing a gator gar in, then placing a hand on its humungousness, making it tangible. And it's also more than the cheering and picture-taking, the measuring and weighing, its release back into the murk, and all the stories that happen after that. It's knowing that they're out there, and that the more I wait it out, watching the warblers and water snakes, the occasional turtle popping up, while enjoying a beer with a friend or two, the more likely the possibility that I'll see a lunker come busting up. Because, as Doug Stange, editor-in-chief of *In-Fisherman*, agrees, "Large alligator gar need immediate protection . . . so generations yet coming can marvel at this monster."[74]

The following four recommendations for preserving and propagating alligator gar in Arkansas (and beyond) are not so much revelations as they are common sense steps that can be considered a basic roadmap for how to proceed from here. In fact, many of the approaches listed below are already happening in Arkansas and other states.

Since there's absolutely no doubt that gar populations are "extremely small and hence quite vulnerable to over exploitation," and are therefore "a species in need of conservation,"[75] it's indisputably obvious that we need immediate action on the local gar front. Regional and national garologists concur that the primary consideration for these imperiled populations is to protect the ones that are already there, in all their various stages of growth.[76] Thus, it's unanimous among gator gar authorities that limiting exploitation is the first major recommendation.

Most experts suggest placing a limit on the taking of gator gar throughout the state as soon as possible, via licensing processes already in place, to which new restrictions can be added later. Layher states, "Either limiting harvest extremely by a trophy tag scenario (perhaps 1 per year) or completely closing the season on alligator gar harvest is recommended."[77] This highly controversial solution (which is one step away from abstinence) essentially echoes Ferrara's assertion that "use of maximum size limits or slot limits . . . would likely have the greatest positive impact on population growth rates depending on the size limit chosen." Ferrara adds, "Creel or effort restrictions and quotas may reduce economic returns and result in closure of commercial fisheries. Closure of seasons or fisheries obviously eliminates or reduces both recreational and commercial fisheries."[78] The implication in this, of course, is that limiting fishing and bowhunting may not be a popular decision, but that's what needs to be done to stave off a total crash of the species.

The second recommendation, which involves designing and implementing a multi-faceted management plan, can be applied simultaneously with putting new restrictions into place. "Re-education," a term employed by Kennedy and successfully utilized by the Missouri Department of Conservation in their recent reintroduction of alligator gar in southeast Missouri, would be the starting point for any management plan focused on bringing the numbers up. Since it's generally agreed by biologists and wildlife officials that it's urgent for gator gar bowhunters to hunt less for the thrill of it and employ more stewardship, this is an extremely vital area in which to concentrate.

As Holt explains, one of the first things that needs to happen "is changing that public misconception" concerning gar. Holt notes how there's a culture of raising kids to believe that "gars are bad things," which gets passed down through generations.[79] Such teachings lead to mass quantities of gar being thrown on the shore, the deliberate breaking off of thousands (if not tens of thousands) of beaks each year, and a general consensus that gar are trash fish that should be viciously exterminated.

Kennedy's Mingo Swamp reintroduction project can be used as a model on how to cut down on the above and approach the implementation of a successful management plan. Before stocking the Mingo Wildlife Management Area, Kennedy's department held public talks for years in and around Cape Girardeau to dispel the many myths about gator gar that led to their devalued reputation. Not only were anglers and bowhunters invited to attend, they were encouraged to participate, and their feedback was incorporated into the management planning. This was all part of a strategy that included programs for school children and the inclusion of various organizations. And Holt, being aware of how well this type of communication worked in Missouri, has similar plans for Arkansas. He states:

> We've talked to several representatives of the bow fishermen of Arkansas and the vibe we're getting from them is that they know something needs to be done. . . [U]sually when we do our regulations we've got to identify all use groups that potentially will oppose the regulation change. And [bow fishermen] would be the biggest one, of course, but I think those guys, because they see what we're trying to do . . . are going to support us . . . What we want to do is come up with a package of options . . . we can have our opinion of what would best benefit [the situation], but we get their input and then we can decide.[80]

But there's another type of communication that needs to be employed in any proposed management plan, which involves a "work locally, think globally" sensibility in coordinating with other states, so that we're all on the same page and working toward the same objectives. Because, as Holt also notes, "We're talking to biologists in Texas and right now they just got a lot of their stuff shot down and the problem with that is . . . because of our regulations. An argument their commission expressed was, 'Why should we be more restrictive on our fishing when surrounding states have more liberal regulations and their populations aren't as good as ours?' So that's a valid argument."[81]

Gar P.R. aside, however, there's another aspect to constructing an effective management plan, which has to do with the actual physical work involved in increasing the size of existing populations. Since Holt recommends "getting the general public on our side and then addressing habitat issues,"[82] the next logical step in a visionary gator gar management plan is to reclaim the natural habitats.

Constructing wetlands and increasing access to marshy areas where the ideal vegetation can flourish is currently the main idea in the reclamation of alligator gar spawning grounds—provided, of course, that floodwater levels can be maintained for the appropriate length of time during spawns. But a water temperature conducive to spawning must also be factored in.

In the Ouachita River beneath the Felsenthal Dam, Layher recommends "The construction of a one to two acre spawning wetland . . . Such an area could be constructed along the old river channel and planted [with] herbaceous wetland vegetation. This would insure spawning habitat even if the river dropped prior to adequate temperatures being reached to entice spawning in the fish."[83] Similarly, Holt recommends converting oxbows into "nurseries": "We've got a potential one I've got in mind over near Brinkley . . . [which] doesn't receive a whole lot of fishing pressure . . . there's plenty of forage fish in there for them, and also, you can go in there . . . and sample for them, see if they're still in there."[84] Such "refuge areas"[85] (like the highly progressive Mingo Wildlife Preserve in Missouri's Bootheel), are what Ferrara recommends to protect alligator gar during all stages of their life cycles.

Once annual spawning grounds are more accessible to gar (and less accessible to humans), "Large scale stocking of alligator gar to overcome the loss of reproductive habitats is one conservation option to restore alligator gar to [their] historical range."[86] Ferrara recommended such stock enhancement for three populations in Louisiana to "re-establish populations of alligator gar that have been extirpated."[87] Kennedy applied this tactic in Missouri, where alligator gar are once again beginning to thrive in the far reaches of Mingo Swamp.

The third recommendation for bringing back alligator gar is to compete even more aggressively for the funding of specific gator gar projects. And in this field, there's a lot of work to be done. As Ferrara indicates, "Because patterns of elasticities are not static for different levels of vital rates, monitoring of vital rates, population growth rates, and elasticity patterns are needed to evaluate the effect of stochastic changes on conservation and management plans."[88] Ferrara also states, "Studies to address ecology and management of early life history stages of alligator gar are needed, particularly because some regions have expressed interest in or have begun stocking small alligator gar to re-establish extirpated populations."[89] Ferrara concludes: "Future research should attempt to validate aging procedures, quantify exploitation rates, quantify juvenile mortality, define habitat usage for all life stages and examine the implications of stocking and stochastic environmental variables. Potential loss of genetic diversity through large-scale stocking efforts should also be assessed. The effectiveness of stocking efforts can be better assessed after the survivability of hatchery-raised individuals is determined and availability and quality of juvenile habitats are determined."[90]

It should also be noted that even though not much commercial fishing for alligator gar happens in Arkansas, it does take place. As Layher informed me, he "talked to a commercial fisherman" who told him that he caught three alligator gar, which "weighed a little over 750 pounds." Layher added, "He's the type of guy [who] doesn't talk a whole lot, but if you get him talking . . . it's pretty legitimate."[91] Meaning Layher considered the man a reliable source.

The point being: Whether by accident or on purpose, Arkansas commercial fishermen still occasionally bag alligator gar; and when this happens, it usually goes unreported. If this data were to be recorded, however, it could definitely be utilized. As Ferrara explains, concerning the situation in Louisiana, where commercial fishing for gator gar is still legal, "Although limiting the number of commercial licenses sold does not prevent increased effort by individual commercial license holders, expansion of the fishery would be prevented. Annual reporting would require commercial anglers to record numbers and total weight of alligator gar harvested. Harvest data could be used for analysis of population trends and could eventually provide a valuable long-term data set." Ferrara recommends employing "mark-recapture studies, in cooperation with commercial anglers, to attempt to estimate population size and to potentially provide insight into alligator gar movement patterns."[92]

Of course, data from anyone who either catches or kills an alligator gar can be used to learn more about the species. Especially if a more extreme cap was set on how many gator gar sportsmen can harvest or catch per year, through a more sophisticated licensing system which encourages the submission of data as an obligation for the privilege of hunting or catching an alligator gar.

As far as research goes, we should also take a more serious look at the idea of gar farming, since it's currently happening in Mexico with great success. Having brought the buffalo back from extinction, to the point where anyone who enters a Ruby Tuesday can order a bison burger, it's possible that alligator gar can also become a valuable food source.

Gar, however, aren't being raised in Mexico by the tens of thousands just for food; they're being raised for research too. What their practical applications are has yet to be determined, but one possibility is that since all gar fry feed on mosquito larvae, this fish could be used for the control of malaria and encephalitis.

As stated earlier, alligator gar might also be applied for rough-fish control, Asian carp control, snakehead eradication, and overall ecological balance. And since alligator gar have recently been pronounced "not guilty" by biologist and "extreme angler" Jeremy Wade to the charges of attacking humans,[93] it would be reasonable to give gator gar a chance to serve us, since we have nothing to lose (including our limbs) and much to gain by serving them.

But for gator gar to serve us, we must first prevent their imminent crash and encourage the species' preservation. Since research will be a key factor in getting this done, organizing organizations will be a major component in acquiring the funding necessary to start taking this highly maligned fish seriously.

The final recommendation, however, is definitely the easiest: Take a kid to where gator gar are—even if they're in an aquarium. It's as simple as that. Because when children see this crazy creature rising and rolling, the diamond pattern of its armor flashing, that fanged head thrashing and gnashing and shaking like a dynamo as it emerges from the depths like a prehistoric dragon fish weighing one hundred, two hundred, three hundred pounds, that's a vision they'll remember forever. And even if that gar doesn't breach, they'll see this in their imaginations, and the result will be exactly the same: It will lead to an awe-inspired respect for this fish. And since powerful visions carry context—like stories, struggles, the work to be done—future generations will be fascinated into action.

If we're lucky, that is. Because when it comes to preserving gator gar, there is no single silver bullet. This is the consensus of the experts, who agree that all the above recommendations need to happen simultaneously and they need to happen now if we're to propagate the Arkansas alligator gar.

Notes

1. Jay Drott, "Timeless Prowler," Publication unknown, Date unknown, 16. A scanned copy of this article is available online at http://www.sptzr.net/pdf/DOC050409.pdf.

2. Lee Holt, interview by author, January 26, 2009, in Little Rock, transcript, 15.

3. Devona Walker, "Chickasaw Works Make History," *The Oklahoman* (Oklahoma City), March 23, 2008.

4. Spiro Mounds artifact database, http://www.spiromounds.com/pages/maces.htm (accessed February 28, 2009).

5. Samuel de Champlain, *The Works of Samuel de Champlain*, vol. 2, ed. H. P. Biggar, trans. John Squair (Toronto: The Champlain Society, 1925), 91-92. Note: Even though Champlain recorded this fish existing in an uncharacteristic northern region, we know it wasn't a longnose gar, since it is described as being "eight to ten feet long" with "a double row of very sharp, dangerous teeth," which are traits unique to alligator gar.

6. Drott, "Timeless Prowler," 16.

7. Phil Carspecken, "Fable of the Billy Gar," *Fishin' Poems and Others* (Burlington, Iowa: Phileo Publishing Company, 1922), 66.

8. "Fishing at the West," *Putnam's Monthly Magazine of American Literature, Science, and Art*, vol. 2, July-December 1853, 434.

9. Carspecken, "Fable of the Billy Gar," 65.

10. George Powers Dunbar, quoted in Jacob L. Wortman, "Ichthyological Papers by George Powers Dunbar, with a Sketch of His Life," *American Naturalist*, vol. 16, May 1882, 384.

11. Charles Burton, "Alligator Gar . . . Fish Terror or Fishery Tool?" *Arkansas Game & Fish Magazine*, vol. 3, no. 1, 1970, 6.

12. Burton, "Alligator Gar," 6.

13. "Capturing the Marauding Arkansas Gar," *Spot Magazine*, vol. 2, no. 4, December 1941, 37.

14. Johnie M. Gray, "My White River Monster," *Sportfishing*, vol. 3, no. 2, September 1966, 13.

15. Carol Griffee, notes ed., *Arkansas Wildlife: A History*, by Keith Sutton. (Fayetteville: University of Arkansas Press, 1998).

16. Don Fuelsch, "Freshwater Monster . . . the Vicious Alligator Gar," *Southern Angler's Guide*, 1961, 16.

17. Joel M. Vance, "Fish for Gar??" *Missouri Conservationist,* vol. 45, no. 8, August 1984, 9.

18. "Fishing at the West," 434.

19. "Fishing at the West," 434.

20. *Fishes and Fishing in Louisiana,* (New Orleans: State of Louisiana Department of Conservation, 1933), 395. This figure is based on the knowledge that on the maiden voyage of the *Electrical Gar Destroyer,* Colonel Burr wiped out seventy-five alligator gar and one thousand turtles.

21. Col. J. G. Burr, ed. *Fishes of Texas,* bulletin no. 5 (Austin: Texas Game, Fish and Oyster Commission, 1932), 40.

22. Col. J. G. Burr, *Conservation of Wildlife Resources,* bulletin no. 9 (Austin: Texas Game, Fish and Oyster Commission, 1935), 1, 7.

23. Col. J. G. Burr, "Electricity as a Means of Garfish and Carp Control," *Transactions of the American Fisheries Society,* vol. 61, no. 1, 1931, 181.

24. Aldo Leopold, "The Role of Wildlife in a Liberal Education," *Transactions of the North American Wildlife Conference,* vol. 7, 1942, 487.

25. Royal D. Suttkus, "Order Lepisostei," *Fishes of the Western North Atlantic,* Memoir Sears Foundation for Marine Research: New Haven. vol. 1, no. 3, 1963, 74.

26. Burt G. Wilder, "Gar-Pikes, Old and Young, [Part] I," *The Popular Science Monthly,* May 1877, 6.

27. "Capturing the Marauding Arkansas Gar," 37.

28. "Capturing the Marauding Arkansas Gar," 37.

29. For example, the Louisiana Department of Conservation claimed, "they are a pest to the commercial fisherman and to the angler alike, for their voracity is responsible for the destruction of great numbers of useful and valuable fishes" *Fishes and Fishing in Louisiana,* 387, 389. Also, according to the State of Illinois, the gar is "a wholly worthless and destructive nuisance in its relations to mankind. It is the enemy of practically all the other fishes in our waters, and so far as it eats anything but fishes, it subtracts from the food supply of the more valuable kinds. It has, in fact all the vices and none of the virtues of a predaceous fish. . . . and by most their destruction is rightly sought" (Stephen Alfred Forbes and Robert Earl Richardson, *The Fishes of Illinois,* 2nd ed., Springfield: State of Illinois, 1920, p. 32).

30. Keith Sutton, "Leviathan Adventure," *North American Fisherman,* vol. 16, no. 7, December 2003/January 2004, 50.

31. Alfred C. Weed, *The Alligator Gar* (Chicago: Field Museum of Natural History, 1923), 66.

32. Dennis L. Scarnecchia, "A Reappraisal of Gars and Bowfins in Fishery Management," *Fisheries,* vol. 17, no. 4, July/August 1992, 11.

33. Robin Huggins, "The Alligator Gar," *Arkansas Wildlife,* Fall 1992, 19.

34. Keith Sutton, "Gar Wars," *In-Fisherman,* March 1998, 49.

35. E. W. Gudger, "Giant Fishes of North America," *Natural History,* February 1942, 118. Incidentally, the * footnote indicates that gasses bloating these fish accounted for extra girth, whereas the † footnote explains that 22.5 pounds of this gar's weight was due to eggs.

36. John Fox, quoted in Sutton, "Gar Wars," 47.

37. John Fox interview by Keith Sutton, November 3, 1997, transcript, 5.

38. Fox, interview by Sutton, 7.

39. John Heuston, interview by Keith Sutton, November 4, 1997, transcript, 1.

40. Bill Apple, quoted in Sutton, *Arkansas Wildlife*, 193.

41. Charley Alter, interview by Keith Sutton, November 4, 1997, transcript, 3.

42. Allyse Marie Ferrara, "Life-History Strategy of Lepisosteidae: Implications for the Conservation and Management of Alligator Gar" (dissertation, Auburn University, 2001), 4.

43. Fox, interview by Sutton, 4.

44. "Capturing the Marauding Arkansas Gar," 37.

45. Larry Drennen Bouchard, e-mail to Keith Sutton, November 23, 2001.

46. Mack Roy, letter to Keith Sutton, September 16, 1993.

47. William G. Layher, et al., "Literature Survey, Status in States of Historic Occurrence, and Field Investigations into the Life History of Alligator Gar in the Ouachita River, Arkansas" (Pine Bluff: Layher BioLogics RTEC, Inc., September 24, 2008), 12.

48. This figure was arrived at through combining: 1) Layher's sampling results in the Ouachita River (which indicated "a population estimate of thirty-one individuals," Layher, "Literature Survey," 26; 2) Dr. Reid Adams's mark-recapture estimate of seventy-five to one hundred individuals in the Fourche LaFave system, personal communication with author, January 2009; and 3) the extreme likelihood that there are less than sixty-nine individuals in the remainder of the state. The word "known," of course, is key in this assessment; there might be other populations we are not aware of yet—and hopefully that's the case.

49. Layher, "Literature Survey," 26.

50. William G. Layher, interview by author in Pine Bluff, January 2009, transcript, 3.

51. Fox, interview by Sutton, 7.

52. Sutton, "Leviathan Adventure," 50.

53. Ferrara, "Life-History Strategy," 12.

54. Ferrara, "Life-History Strategy," 58.

55. Keith Sutton, "Adventures: Choke Canyon, Texas, Gators," *In-Fisherman*, vol. 24, no. 7, December 1999/January 2000, 28.

56. Huggins, "The Alligator Gar," 19.

57. William G. Layher, e-mail to Keith Sutton, January 14, 1999.

58. Layher, interview by author, 3.

59. Edward Kluender, interview by author in Conway, January 2009, transcript, 1.

60. Layher, interview by author, 5.

61. Lee Holt, quoted in Randy Zellers, "Rough Fish Wanted," *Arkansas Wildlife*, May/June 2009, 19.

62. Scarnecchia, "A Reappraisal of Gars," 10.

63. Weed, *The Alligator Gar*, 10.

64. Scarnecchia, "A Reappraisal of Gars," 10.

65. Scarnecchia, "A Reappraisal of Gars," 5.

66. James Nelson Gowanloch, "Control of Gar Fish in Louisiana," *Transactions of the North American Wildlife Conference*, vol. 5, 1940, 293.

67. Scarnecchia, "A Reappraisal of Gars," 10.

68. Holt, interview by author, 12. Incidentally, Holt credits this scenario to biologist Christopher Kennedy of the Missouri Department of Conservation.

69. Holt, interview by author, 12.

70. Scarnecchia, "A Reappraisal of Gars," 10.

71. Christopher Kennedy, interview by author, Cape Girardeau, Missouri, April 2005. Also see Mark Spitzer, "In Search of Massive Missouri Gar," *Rougarou*, vol. 2, no. 1, http://www.louisiana.edu/Academic/LiberalArts/EngL/Creative/Rougarou/currentIssue/Spitzer_missouriGar.html, Fall 2008.

72. See http://www.youtube.com/watch?v=DjOZ7GBw654 (accessed May 1, 2009).

73. Weed, *The Alligator Gar*, 12.

74. Doug Stange, "A Monster in Appearance and Proportion," *In-Fisherman*, April 1996, 11.

75. Layher, "Literature Survey," i, 1.

76. Layer, "Literature Survey," 27. Layher's field investigation into the life history of Ouachita River alligator gar concludes, "Firstly affording protection to the existing numbers should be a high priority." Ferrara, "Life-History Strategy," 52. Ferrara's dissertation on the implications for gator gar conservation and management concurs, "All life history stages should be protected."

77. Layher, "Literature Survey," 27.

78. Ferrara, "Life-History Strategy," 54.

79. Holt, interview by author, 13.

80. Holt, interview by author, 4.

81. Holt, interview by author, 5.

82. Holt, interview by author, 13.

83. Layher, "Literature Survey," 27.

84. Holt, interview by author, 13.

85. Ferrara, "Life-History Strategy," 52.

86. Ferrara, "Life-History Strategy," 58.

87. Ferrara, "Life-History Strategy," 56.

88. Ferrara, "Life-History Strategy," 52.

89. Ferrara, "Life-History Strategy," 62.

90. Ferrara, "Life-History Strategy," 64.

91. Layher, interview by author, 1.

92. Ferrara, "Life-History Strategy," 56.

93. After evidence was presented that gar do not eat what they cannot swallow whole, and that they hold their food while assessing if the size of the prey merits releasing, fishing show host Jeremy Wade concludes that "Gar have neither the power nor the attitude for premeditated violent attacks on humans." "Alligator Gar," *River Monsters* (Bristol, United Kingdom: Icon Films, 2009), Animal Planet.

14

Long Live the Gar!

IT WAS AN ENCOURAGING DAY in gator gar history: May 29, 2009. When I got down to the main Arkansas Game & Fish office in Little Rock, there were about eighteen bowhunters (plus a few wives and children) assembled in the auditorium. They were all sitting on one side of the room, and two UCA graduate students in biology, Ed Kluender and Tommy Inebnit, were on the other, along with three-fourths of the state's newly established Alligator Gar Species Management Team: Lee Holt, Eric Brinkman, and Jimmy Barnett. So I signed in, grabbed a free gar-identification poster (since Game & Fish was kicking off its statewide gar-education program), and took a seat over by the biologists.

There was definitely a tension in the air. It was the second meeting Game & Fish had called with local bow fishermen, who were now being asked to provide input and vote on options for protecting alligator gar. The first option was a complete moratorium on the harvest of all gator gar in the state for five years—which wasn't very likely. The second was a one-alligator-gar-per-day limit in conjunction with a free permit. And the third was a two-gator-gar-per-day limit that went along with buying a special tag. For the last two options, the license (for bowhunting as well as rod and reel) would be good for the entire season, except from the middle of April to the middle of June, when alligator gar spawn in Arkansas.

The discussion started and the bowshooters made their concerns clear. They were glad to protect alligator gar, since they were going for shortnose anyway. They were tournament hunters, but sometimes they accidentally shot small gator gar, because they're hard to tell from shortnose in the water. In fact, they even claimed to have shot some sixteen-inchers, a size that Game & Fish and the UCA biologists had been trying to sample for years without success. Mainly, though, the shortnose shooters were concerned about getting busted if alligator gar became protected.

That's when the word "incidental" came up. Game & Fish had inserted this word into the options to protect anyone who might accidentally shoot a small gator gar. If someone shot a five-foot alligator gar, however, there'd be no way this word could protect him. So that's what the discussion concerned.

Game & Fish said that what they wanted was data, so they wouldn't get upset if the tournament hunters turned in any incidental gar. In fact, they'd rather have those gar turned in than discarded, so they could get more statistics on record.

On the bowhunting side, most of the talking was done by this guy who another bowhunter announced was the president of the Bowhunting Association of America. The president said that their group didn't target alligator gar, and that the guys who went for the big ones were "weekend warriors." Meaning the shortnose shooters found it important to distinguish themselves from those who hunted gator gar specifically, none of whom were present that night.

"Besides," the president added, "when someone gets an alligator gar, we all hear about it. There's never more than a dozen a year."

"That you know of . . ." a Game & Fish agent added.

Then came the question regarding how many people rod-and-reel fished for gator gar in the state. Nobody could answer this, but I knew I was one of them—perhaps the only one. I didn't raise my hand, though, because the way I figured it . . . the less the better. Besides, I was there to observe, not complicate the matter further.

Anyhow, the more we talked, the more we all discovered we were there for the same reason: Which wasn't really as much about not getting ticketed as it was "To manage and restore alligator gar populations in suitable waters of their historic range throughout Arkansas while providing a unique sport fishery." That's the objective Brinkman's PowerPoint presentation was projecting on the screen. And since we had this mutual goal, the defensiveness, I think, dissipated, the conversation became constructive, and eventually, the bowhunters agreed on the second option: one per day on a free permit—to ensure that more catches and kills get reported, because if Arkansans are forced to buy a special permit, the bowshooters reckoned, they'd be less likely to report any incidental gar. That was the mindset, so we got on to the next subject: reporting them.

The bow fishermen were given four options: A) After shooting one, call up Game & Fish and make a report within twenty-four hours; B) make keeping a fishing diary part of the deal when you get a permit; C) distribute a mandatory annual survey with every permit application; or D) make reporting gator gar information for the previous season a prerequisite for renewing a tag. And to my surprise, they didn't choose just one option— they chose three out of four. The diary idea got the boot.

"We want to help y'all get your information," the president told us, and we moved on to the next discussion: designating some specific gator gar refuges.

The proposal was: "It shall be unlawful to take or attempt to take *any* alligator gar while fishing in Pool [X] of the Arkansas River . . . , the Ouachita River downstream of Felsenthal Lock and Dam, and any associated tributaries within these areas."

Leaning forward, I whispered to Ed, "Does this mean our gar could be totally protected?"

He nodded in the affirmative, flashing me a quirky grin—which basically meant that our local population would be protected throughout the year.

"Uh, I don't know about that," one of the bow fishermen put in. "I know about ten or fifteen guys who aren't going to be very happy about that."

At this point, I couldn't contain myself. Since those ten or fifteen guys are exactly who we need to protect those seventy-five to a hundred gator gar from, I piped out:

"Well, they aren't here adding their voice to the conversation, so it's up to you to decide if you want those gar protected."

The bowhunters agreed. Earlier that month, in the area under discussion, someone had shot a six-footer and just left it there. The shortnose shooters, however, had pressured the guy to report the fish, which took a couple of days, but eventually it happened. Apparently, the UCA biologists had caught this one three times in one of their gill nets and had attached a radio transmitter to it, but then some good old boy had come along and done it in, while it was swimming around in the shallows. There were a bunch of different stories circulating about how it died, and the rumors were already starting to fly since everyone's on the Internet now and has cell phones as well.

And that was it: Three major options had been decided, so now Game & Fish could take these decisions to the next level, say this is what the people want, and hopefully next year there'll be some new regulations.

The meeting was adjourned and the groups came together: biologists and bowhunters, Game & Fish agents, and some obscure gar-writer no one ever heard of. E-mails were exchanged so pictures of the big dead one could be sent around, and everyone started talking fishing. And archery.

And telling each other where they'd seen the eight-footers—info that gator gar hunters keep to themselves.

"They're a strange breed," Ed told me. "They don't come out to talk about stuff like this. They want to keep their hunting spots private."

"There's some guys down by Felsenthal Dam," a bowhunter told us, "who put their trolling motors right over those buoys and go in after them."

"We're going to keep an eye out for them," Brinkman said.

I turned to Holt, and asked him about the fourth member of the management team, Ricky Campbell in Mississippi:

"Does having a hatchery specialist being part of this process means that if these regulations go forth you hope to start stocking?"

"Yup," he replied. "Usually Game & Fish doesn't like to recruit from out of state, but we put the idea forth, and they went for it with no hesitation."

But it was also a discouraging day in gar history. Because talking with Ed, who monitors the movements of alligator gar, I asked him where our local ones were—since I'd been out there for the last few months and hadn't seen hide nor hair. He told me that they'd gone into the Arkansas, and that three of them had mysteriously disappeared. Only their transmitters were recovered in a ditch by the spawning grounds. Someone had removed them.

This meant that at least three members of the largest-known gator gar population in the state had been dispatched of during the spawning season. This also meant that since there's a lot of gator gar harvest that goes unreported, at least 3 to 4 percent of a population I had personally helped tag had most likely been left for the crows. And since it's highly probable that the one the shortnose shooters pressured the guy to call in was from the same population (since they all went down in the same place), this basically raised the statistic to 5 or 6 percent snuffed within the last few weeks. Needless to say, the loss of those gars came as a heavy blow to me.

"A lot of those guys," another bowhunter added, "don't even use arrows. They just shoot 'em with guns and leave 'em there. I know a lot of those boys, and law or no law, they ain't gonna change their ways."

"Damn," I replied, and walked out to my car, not knowing whether to be heartened by the progress that night, or bummed out at how easy it is to just watch it all get flushed away.

Last Christmas, or maybe it was my birthday, my wife gave me a DVD titled *Let 'm Roll!* My response was an immediate groan, because I'd heard about the Gar Guys before—who, according to the packaging, produced "The most awesome big gar bow fishing video ever!"

A filmmaker named Scott Perry in Austin had contacted me back in 2007 about an "effort underway to immediately stop the harvesting of the last giant alligator gar in Texas's rivers." Perry explained how a "quasi-legal practice called bowhunting, led by professional for-profit expedition hosts who know where the secret breeding nests are for these ancient females," were gearing up to bring trophy hunters into the spawning grounds on the weekends of May 5 and May 12. This e-mail contained a link to an article posted on the *Austin Statesman* website (it has since been taken down due to the controversy it generated), which described how the commercial guides known as the Gar Guys get up in the morning, pray to the Lord for luck in killing endangered Texas alligator gar, then take non-Texans into the spawning grounds, where they shoot as many as they can for thousands of dollars.

Perry's e-mail also contained a blurb from Bill Layher, who noted: "I spent four years trying to sample alligator gar in Arkansas. While people occasionally get a few, our efforts resulted in a grand total of four fish, the largest being 157 lbs. I believe they are not reproducing much in Arkansas and what we have are the remains of a population represented by a few relic old fish. I have literally expended thousands of net nights on Arkansas's large rivers since 1995 and have only caught one juvenile alligator gar which was in the Ouachita just above the La. border."

Gar specialist Elise Irwin of Auburn University was then quoted as saying, "alligator gar are imperiled throughout their range and conservation efforts are underway in most areas. I guess TX and LA are still behind on this effort."

This information was followed by an analysis from an "expert at Tishomongo National Fish Hatchery in Oklahoma," who asserted that there are "probably very few giant gar in Texas."

That's why I groaned. Given that sportfishing, bowhunting, shooting gar en masse, and just conking the big ones on their heads had exacerbated the damage done by dams in Arkansas, I didn't think I could watch that DVD. Especially after what the historic guide John Fox said about fishing for gator gar back in the '50s: "[W]e were catching these gar like there was never a tomorrow. When we got one to the boat, we'd shoot it and just let it sink. We thought we were doing a great service. We were told they'd eat their weight in game fish every forty-eight hours. So if it was a 150-pounder, you could look at 150 pounds of fish going out of the river every two days. We thought we were getting rid of all these predators, but, in fact, we were victims of our own greed . . . just five years after I started, I had to quit . . . The gar were gone."

Nevertheless, I kept that DVD around, thinking that maybe there'd be something I could learn from it, even if I didn't agree with the Ted Nugent mentality of "Bowfishin' is a riot!! Kill 'em all!!"

So finally I decided to watch it, and I found it to be just as disturbing as I expected it to be. *Let 'm Roll* opened with the Gar Guys shooting blindly into a river full of roiling gar, not knowing for certain the size or species they were shooting at. Sometimes they'd put an arrow or two into a big one, then fight it till it broke away, bleeding to death. Whereas it's the norm for hunters to go after wounded deer, though, the Gar Guys didn't worry themselves with such ethics. They just kept shooting.

Talk about fish in a barrel! Those Gar Guys would find a spot where hundreds of gar were rolling on the surface, then pull their boat into the thick of it. They'd shoot them up and haul them in, gar after gar after gar after gar. Five-footers, six-footers, seven-footers, as many as they could Kill Kill Kill! They even busted the jaw on a two-hundred-pounder, while laughing at it, giving each other high fives, and calling it "Pig!"

In just one day on the Trinity River, the Gar Guys destroyed four gator gar over two hundred pounds and quite a few more over a hundred, while hooting and hollering and slapping each other on the back. And though I saw the Gar Guys eating fried gar, I find it doubtful that they really had freezer space for the twenty giant gar (that's at least a ton of meat!) they posed with on the front and back cover of the DVD. Especially since it's common knowledge that the big ones are full of insecticides, PCBs, DDT, mercury, lead, etc. And as most fishermen know, the younger fish have less chemicals in them—which is undoubtedly why the Gar Guys chose a three-footer for their instructional part on how to clean an alligator gar. This was the only useful moment in a video in which thousands of pounds of gar meat and gar-life went to waste.

Then, at the end of the segment, the Gar Guys talked about how they'd been blessed by God. For the gar they smeared to death, however, the story was the exact opposite.

That kind of stuff really burns me up! I mean, how vain it is to use religion to justify the destruction of an awesome creature like the alligator gar, and how infuriating it is to see those bozos mass-executing gar the age of their grandmothers just because they can. But that's nothing new in America, where there's always been a battle between those who believe that God wants man to kill "ugly fish," and those who believe that if God exists, He would never condone such a thing.

Whatever the case, I truly believe that at the core of all our gar-tensions there's a fundamental clash of cultures that will never be resolved. From the settlers who tried to eliminate what they couldn't understand, to the damming of a continent in order to establish a shoot-first-ask-questions-later cowboy mentality (which isn't always as compassionate as it professes to be), to clowns like the Gar Guys killing gar for "sport," I see myself as a bitter witness to an unconscionable stewardship.

Plus, you'd think that the Gar Guys would be aware of passages in the Bible like Genesis 1:20–21, wherein it is written: "God created fish . . . And God said, 'let the water teem with living creatures' . . . And God saw that it was good."

So if God created alligator gar, and if alligator gar are "good" (as well as an officially threatened species), then a pox upon those who profit off the blood of gar and drive their numbers down! Especially when they refuse to acknowledge previous mistakes. As Keith Sutton notes in a garticle subtitled "Lessons Not Learned," "There is a lesson to be learned here . . . If only we had known then what we know now."

The thing is, with what we do know now about how easy it is to obliterate entire gator gar populations, we still allow guys like the Gar Guys to wipe them out like they're going out of style. And they are.

Given that world fish populations are currently being decimated on a daily basis, there's no guarantee that our most endangered gar species won't suddenly go the way of the Pacific salmon. In the last few years, millions of wild salmon have suddenly disappeared from the west coast of North America, from Canada down to Mexico. Abnormal weather patterns are to blame, along with dams, development, insecticides, and factors that have yet to be determined. Most of these elements, of course, are also the major contributors to declining gator gar populations.

In British Columbia's Strait of Georgia, sport fishermen caught one million Coho in 1988. Twenty years later, those numbers are down to less than ten thousand per year. In the Sacramento River in California, the Chinook run has dropped from roughly nine hundred thousand to fifty-six thousand in just six years. That's a 94 percent drop in that population, and some fishery managers confirm that these "salmon may already be commercially extinct." Hence, a federal ban on commercial salmon fishing has been established from Washington State to Southern California, economies are in peril, and it's not very likely that the devastated populations will be coming back in the near future.

And don't even get me started on sturgeon. According to Richard Adams Carey's *The Philosopher Fish: Sturgeon, Caviar and the Geography of Desire* (2005), "sturgeon populations worldwide have declined seventy percent in the last twenty years."

In other words, ecosystems are collapsing all around us, we are in the midst of a cataclysmic environmental crisis, and no one seems to be sounding the alarm. Today it's salmon and sturgeon, tomorrow it could be gar—which is why we need to be a lot more careful with preserving what's left. Otherwise, what happened with alligator gar in Arkansas could happen in Texas in only one or two seasons. It's happened before, it's happening now, and without gator gar to control big minnow populations, the number of rough fish could increase exponentially, annihilating thousands of acres of gamefish-nesting habitats virtually overnight. And even if it takes years for the ecological balance to completely crash in the state of Texas, the results will be exactly the same.

Thinking about Texas, where the largest populations of gator gar still exist, sent me to the Internet. Recently, there'd been a lot of brouhaha in that state regarding changes in alligator gar restrictions, so I began Googling. It didn't take long to find out that a new statewide law would soon be going into effect. According to the Texas Parks and Wildlife website, the regulations were scheduled to "change Sept. 1, 2009, from no length or daily bag limit to a one fish per day bag limit. The bag will apply to both recreational and commercial fishing."

"Alright!" I shouted, because this meant that next year, if all went according to plan, both Arkansas and Texas would have a one-gator-gar-per-day limit. A one-gator-gar-per-season limit would be ideal, but this was a start. Besides, it's pretty much common knowledge that since getting one per day (much less one per season) in Arkansas is a rare event, getting more than one is twice as unlikely. Still, the possibility existed that an Arkie could get more than one in a day, but the possibility also existed that the laws could be tightened up later.

Texas, however, was another story. Some of the bowshooters at the Game & Fish meeting told me that it had been a highly controversial decision over there. Like the Arkansas Game & Fish Commission, Texas Parks and Wildlife had called public meetings with bowhunters, who had put their trust in the state. I don't know the specific details, but I was told that the Texas gator-gar-shooters didn't get what they wanted, so now they were mad as hell.

And I could see how they would be. Not only are there guys over there who go out and shoot alligator gar all day, there are also rod-and-reel and archery guides who depend on multiple one-hundred-plus-pounders to earn their daily crust. Like the commercial fisherman from Mercedes who harvested 38,200 pounds of gator gar last year. That's nearly four hundred gar weighing about a hundred pounds removed from the rivers by just one person! Plus, there's a commercial fishing industry in Texas that processes alligator gar into "pressed fish." Like pot smokers in the United States whose habits create a demand for Mexican shwagg and all the violence that comes from smuggling, it could be posited that the Catholic demand for fish during Lent drives a similar bloodshed for gar.

That's just speculation, though, so I'll stop right there and just mention one more thing about Texas: A closure on all alligator gar harvest in the Hagerman National Wildlife Refuge was put into effect in September 2009 to protect that spawning population.

YAHOOOOO!

Then Googling on, I discovered a recent document titled "Life History and Status of Alligator Gar *Atractosteus spatula,* with Recommendations for Management" by David L. Buckmeier of the Texas Parks and Wildlife Department Inland Fisheries, which provided the following information: "Of the 14 states once inhabited by alligator gar, six consider them to be extremely rare or extirpated . . . In most of these states, alligator gar are not managed; however, Tennessee is now restocking fish and does not allow harvest. Five additional states (i.e., Alabama, Arkansas, Florida, Mississippi, and Oklahoma) have enacted daily creel regulations from 0–2 fish/day . . . In addition to daily creel regulations, Oklahoma has also closed a known spawning area to alligator gar fishing during the spawning season. Several states have stocked or are considering stocking alligator gar."

And not too long after that: "In Texas, increased fishing pressure for alligator gar and future degradation of river and estuarine habitats potentially threaten existing alligator gar populations. Observed declines in other states and vulnerability to overfishing indicate a conservative approach is warranted until populations and potential threats can be fully assessed. It is recommended that the TPWD join other states in managing alligator gar populations by significantly reducing harvest and protecting spawning and nursery areas."

I contacted Buckmeier and found out that this document, among others, was used to make a case for changing the gator gar laws in Texas—

just like Reid Adam's data was used by Arkansas Game & Fish to lessen the pressure on the big ones in my own neighborhood. To this I would add that I saw Reid just the other day at a mind-numbing meeting for grant managers at our university, after which he told me, "Ya know, beyond all the publications that'll come from that research, what I'm most proud about is that our information is going to protect those gar. That's what means the most to me."

But that's a flashback, and in the present tense I am still Googling to find out how alligator gar are faring in other states. What I find is this:

- Alabama has a one-fish-per-day limit and no commercial fishery. They are currently drafting a management plan.
- In Florida, no harvest is allowed, because the extremely small gator gar population is on the decline.
- As for Georgia, nobody knows. There are no regulations on alligator gar and their status in very rare.
- Both Illinois and Indiana have no regulations and gator gar are most likely extirpated.
- Louisiana has no regulations except for an area on the Sabine River. The status is unknown there, but I just read an article about a commercial fisherman in Homa who harvests gator gar every day. Research is on the rise.
- In Missouri, where alligator gar are now being stocked, and where just a few years ago it was thought that they were gone forever, there's a fifty-fish-per-day limit. What's up with that?
- Mississippi has a two-gator-gar-limit per day with some areas closed for harvest. Status unknown.
- There are no regulations in Ohio, but probably also no alligator gar.
- Like Texas and Alabama, there's a daily one-fish limit in Oklahoma. No commercial fishery is allowed, Lake Texoma is closed during spawning season, and a management plan is in the works.
- As stated earlier, no harvest is allowed in Tennessee, which is in need of serious management, even though a plan has been completed. Alligator gar have been reintroduced.

So basically, that's where we're at.

But back to the Arkansas alligator gar, which I'd been trying to catch to no avail. For months, I'd been out there with chunks of drum and frozen grass carp and checking out the flooded fields—but hadn't seen any. When it wasn't raining, that is.

May 2009 had been the wettest May in the state since 1893. There'd been thunderstorms, lightning storms, hail storms, tornado storms, constant drizzle, and slugs all over the strawberries. Lake Conway had flooded our yard, the Toad Suck Dam was completely under water, and we couldn't get our new septic tank installed until the lawn dried out.

In general, all this water was an annoyance for humans. But not for gar, who, on average, only get conditions like this once a decade. Or, in this case, once per century. And since it usually takes seven years for a male to reach breeding age, and eleven years for females to start ovulating, they'd been waiting years for this. The fields had been flooded for weeks and the timing was right for all of the factors to converge. Still, I wasn't that sure about the water temperature, which was still pretty cold, thanks to the continuous rains.

According to Ed Kluender, the big ones had moved out of their tributary and into the Arkansas. According to the bow fishermen, they were going into the spawning grounds. And according to Reid Adams, these dwindling spawning grounds were all that was left of the traditional spawning grounds of gator gar in our region.

So I went out there to check it out, went upstream about a mile, and turned into a backwater: I had tried to access this area the weekend before, but couldn't get to it from the road due to too much private property.

There was just something about this spot on my map. That backwater was full of inlets and bays, so I figured it would also be full of flooded fields. But when I got in there, the banks were high and muddy and there weren't any flooded fields at all. Nor any gator gar rolling. Just gorgeous stretches of sandy spits and over-hanging vines, poison ivy and frightened turtles plopping off logs. Water snakes were everywhere, as were blue herons, spiraling hawks, the occasional breaching smaller gar, and not a cloud in the sky.

I kept on working my way upstream, then came to a bunch of tide pools. Or what looked like tide pools, carved in the bright white sand. So I pulled up on the beach. The water level had been going down, and there was a small stream going through a system of puddles, no doubt coming from another cove. I got out and walked around in the clear pools, which ranged from a few inches deep to two feet deep, and were full of waterbugs and tiny crawfish skittering around.

Then suddenly . . . a micro-gar! I saw it swimming on the surface, looking like a twig with fins. It was so small I could hardly even see it . . . not more than an inch long. But I got my hands under it, lifted, and HOLY COW!, caught it.

It was a longnose. I could tell just by looking at it: the shape of its beak, its skinniness. I put it in the bailing bucket, where it tooled around, shimmying that juvenile tail-spike all baby gar have, which eventually diminishes.

Walking along, I saw more and more. They were in these pools, feeding off the minnows and mosquito larvae. And they were easy to catch by hand. You just slowly approach one from straight ahead (a direction they cannot see), keep your shadow from falling on it, then gradually move your hands in from the sides, cup, and lift. But what worked even better was hiding my hands beneath the sand, then lifting the sand and then the gar. In no time at all, I had eight or nine. Some might have been shortnose, some might have been spotted.

And then I saw it . . . three inches long, just out of its black stage with that gold stripe running down its back, all silvery with leopard spots and that blunt wide head—a definite alligator gar!

I recognized it immediately. I'd caught them in Texas about this size, and had even raised one in a tank. That one got about ten inches long, but then it died. I was pretty depressed when that happened. Never felt that crummy about losing a pet fish before. Always wanted to get another.

And there it was: A highly endangered Arkansas alligator gar, just treading there. Meaning that there were thousands in these waters (which will hopefully be protected next year) just chilling out in pools like this.

I must've whooped, I can't remember. All I know is I went for it. Gator Gar Jr., however, was faster than the others. It shot off—got away.

But I was glad. Because if I can spook it, then other predators will spook it too. And hopefully its siblings will be just as speedy. Because during the next few weeks, they will need sharp eyes and velocity to evade the catfish, the coons, the water birds—and for decades after that, humans who shoot to kill.

It would be foolish, however, to be left with hope just from witnessing that little fish. That's what I told myself, because I wasn't ready to *not* feel defensive. There was still a lot of work to do—in the form of research, education, stories to tell, imaginations to provoke.

In fact, I felt even more responsible now, knowing that the young were out there and growing in our midst. Especially since it will be years before we have more floods like this.

But maybe not. Because now that erratic climate changes are more common than they used to be (thanks to a shift in the jet stream), extreme flooding is becoming more common. And devastating to "civilization."

In most cultures, creation legends start with a flood. The Judeo-Christian idea of Noah and the ark—or a boat full of animals being preserved by an angry God looking out for animals—dates back to *The Gilgamesh Epic,* more than four thousand years ago. The Mesopotamians thought of it first and recorded the story on tens of thousands of clay tablets. Many Native American tribes, though, also have stories about animals on boats. With the Chippewa, there's a bunch of creatures stranded on a raft, looking for a place to land. These animals are told to dive down and grab some mud to bring up to the Trickster figure, who breathes on it to create land for them to live on.

And ironically or not, that's what we're facing now. Our ice shelves are dissolving at the rate of 10 percent every decade and top scientists agree that we won't have any polar caps left in a century. The National Oceanic and Atmospheric Administration and the Intergovernmental Panel on Climate Change (made up of three hundred international scientists) project that temperatures will increase seven to thirteen degrees Fahrenheit in the coming hundred years. And the result, of course, will be what it has always been.

The oceans will rise, washing stuff away—like Florida, Louisiana, and the Netherlands, just for starters. Then there's coastal Alaska, Venice, etc. And gradually, the apocalypse will keep on coming. It happens every ice age—a worldwide chain of cataclysms—with only certain species being able to adapt. Like gar, which can live in both fresh and saltwater, as well as warm and cold water—which is why Arkansas longnose swim with the catfish down in the Delta just as much as they run with the trout up in the Ozarks.

For the time being, though, I'll try to do what we all do: Deny the changes we are facing and act as if there are no irreversible conditions threatening to erase all that we know. But during this denial, I'll focus on what we know: The fact that, while we're here, we can make changes to protect what we care about.

That's the fight I choose, and this is how I choose to do it. I'm sure there are more effective methods, but that's not the way I roll as we all flounder, searching for something that can make us feel existentially useful. Some choose God, I choose Gar. Others choose Hummers, bowhunting, hydrology, whatever. Big deal. As if it matters. We're all going down, we're all going to die.

Gar, however, will survive.

Sure, the largest of the species is on the brink, and could very well be lost if we fail to respect them and ourselves, but the smaller species will endure. You just can't kill them off. We've tried it before, and it's never worked.

And since more flooding means more gar, and since gar have a proven record of enduring eons of whatever this planet can dish out, gar aren't just some incidental "throwback" to the past—gar are the fish of the future. More than any other fish, gar are prepared to fight on, adapt away, and crawl from the muck again. So Viva the Post-Apocalyptic Gar, Viva the Gar in our waters now, and Viva the Gar in all of us—which exist whether we like it or not. Because ultimately, we are all interconnected: humans, mammals, insects, birds, all the creatures—including the coolest fish there is.

Gar Recipes

This is just a sampling of recipes for gar, which have a dense meat that often cooks up thick like chicken. Garfish recipes from Europe, Australia, and New Zealand depend on an entirely different species. North and South American gar meat, however, can be used in almost any recipe that requires a firm, non-oily fish. Gar meat is best served fresh.

The following recipes come from various books as well as the Internet. Since there are quite a few versions of similar recipes in the public domain, I have synthesized some, innovated on others, and have edited the following so that they do not read exactly like their original sources. I have tweaked a few recipes to read more logically, and I have made others more ambiguous on purpose. In some instances, specific measurements are given; in others, the cook will just have to figure out the measurements according to his or her taste and/or the number of people being served. Only the *ceviche* recipe is my own invention. The tempura is always excellent, but the Thai recipe is my favorite.

Versions of these recipes can be found in *The Joy of Cooking,* or on cajun-recipes.com, louisianacajun.com, bassonhook.com, cooks.com, bow.fishingcountry.com, and realcajunrecipes.com.

As for cleaning gar, for a small one (less than three feet), this is the method that works best for me: Using a sharp knife, a tin-snips, and gloves, make a horizontal cut underneath the dorsal fin and snip it off. Remove the fin below that as well so that you can make two lengthwise cuts from the back of the head to the base of the tail; one on the top and one on the bottom of the fish. Then make two perpendicular cuts behind the gills so that you can place the knife along the spine and cut toward the tail, creating two armored filets. Snip off the two middle fins and angle the tip of the knife between the scales and the meat so that you can work the blade along the inside of the armor (from top to bottom works best) and peel the meat away as you go. There's a long strip of backbone muscle above the spine, which may or may not stay with the carcass. Make sure you pull that out and throw it out with the guts. The eggs are poison, so watch out for cats and dogs.

For a large gar (more than three feet), nail the head to a board that's bigger than the fish. Then, using a hatchet or an axe, chop under the top fin toward the head and cut a strip along the backbone. Use a knife and gloves to cut the flesh away from the scales, working your way around its girth with your fingers to release the meat. Chop the spine behind the head, pull out the meat, gut, then cut along backbone muscle and spine to create two big slabs of meat.

You can also cut a whole gar into segments (one- to two-inches thick) with an electric saw, then use a knife to cut along the inside of the armor until the steaks pop out.

Basic Gar Boulettes

> 1 to 3 pounds gar meat, de-boned
> 2 onions, chopped
> 1 cup bread crumbs
> ½ cup chopped fresh parsley
> ½ cup chopped green onions
> 1 or 2 deseeded hot peppers (or a tablespoon or three of cayenne pepper)
> Black pepper
> Salt
> 2 eggs, beaten
> ½ cup cooking oil
> 3 cups water (or half water, half white wine or beer)
> Flour for coating
> Cooked rice

In a food processor, grind up meat, one onion, bread crumbs, parsley, green onions, hot peppers, salt and black pepper (just a pinch of each), and beaten eggs. Form mixture into golf ball-sized balls, then roll in flour and place in hot cooking oil until brown. Remove and stir the remaining chopped onion into the pan and brown. Add water, stir, and put the boulettes back in. Simmer uncovered for 45 minutes. Serve with sauce over rice.

Basic Stir-Fried Gar

5 to 6 pounds gar meat, de-boned, and sliced into 3-inch chunks
1 onion, chopped
1 tablespoon ketchup
1 tablespoon hot sauce
1 tablespoon soy sauce
½ cup cooking oil
Salt
Pepper
3 cups water (or half water, half white wine or beer)
Vegetables (optional)
Cooked rice

Heat oil, add gar chunks and brown. Add onion and stir until lightly browned. Add the ketchup, hot sauce, soy sauce, salt and pepper, and stir lightly. Add water, cover, and simmer for 45 minutes. If you want to add vegetables (e.g., broccoli, carrots, peas, mushrooms), chop them up and throw them in for the last fifteen minutes. Serve over rice.

Basic Gar Cakes

About 4 pounds gar meat, de-boned and chopped
5 or 6 medium potatoes, boiled and mashed
5 or 6 green onions, chopped
1 onion, chopped
½ green pepper, chopped
3 to 6 cloves of garlic, chopped
2 eggs, beaten
Hot sauce to taste
1 tablespoon salt
1 teaspoon black pepper
Flour for coating
¼ cup cooking oil

Mix all ingredients (except flour and cooking oil) in food processor and pat into 4- to 5-inch cakes. Flour cakes and place in hot oil until golden brown.

Basic Gar Stew

    1½ to 2 pounds gar filets
    ¾ to 1 cup flour
    1 teaspoon salt
    ½ teaspoon black pepper
    3 tablespoons butter or margarine
    3 tablespoons olive oil
    3 cups hot water (part wine or beer is fine)
    ⅛ teaspoon cayenne pepper (or more)
    ½ teaspoon black pepper
    ½ teaspoon thyme
    4 potatoes, cubed
    4 onions, chopped
    3 carrots, chopped

Coat filets in flour and heat olive oil in large pan. Brown gar filets one minute on each side. Pour hot water in a stew pot, and add cayenne, salt, pepper, thyme, potatoes and onions. Cover and simmer hard for 10 minutes. Add carrots and cook for 10 minutes or until tender. Drain and save water. Place gar filets in casserole dish, add vegetables, and pour the water over it all. Cover and bake at 350 degrees for 45 minutes.

Basic Mississippi Gar

    1 slab of gar meat (ideally, bigger than a large steak)
    2 cups ketchup
    ¼ cup hot sauce
    ½ cup celery, chopped
    1 onion, chopped
    4 tablespoons soy sauce
    ½ cup green onions, chopped
    1 tablespoon salt
    2 teaspoons black pepper
    2 cups water
    Lemon

Mix everything except the fish and lemon in a casserole dish. Add meat, cover, and marinate in refrigerator all afternoon. Then stir up the saucy stuff and cook at 400 degrees for 1 hour, turning the meat a couple of times and covering with sauce. Squeeze lemon over gar before serving.

Captain Bill's Balls

De-boned gar meat, no gelatinous tissue
Boiled potatoes (equal in weight to gar meat)
½ cup green onions, finely chopped
¼ to ½ cup shallots, chopped
Corn flour (not cornmeal or white flour)
Crawfish- or crab-boil mix
Egg
Milk

Wrap gar meat in cheesecloth and boil in the crawfish-boil mix until flaky white. Unwrap gar meat and combine with shallots, green onions and potatoes in food processor. Mix until you are able to form firm patties. Dip into mixture of a beaten egg with a splash of milk, then dredge in corn flour. Deep fry at 350 degrees for 8 to 10 minutes. Serve with cold beer!

Grilled Gar Patties

3 pounds gar meat
2 medium onions, minced
2 cups bread crumbs
2 eggs, beaten
2 tablespoons paprika
2 tablespoons chili powder
Salt
Pepper

Combine all ingredients. Run through food processor and form into patties. Place on grill and baste with a mixture of the following:

2 tablespoons sugar
2 cups ketchup
Juice of 2 lemons
1 tablespoon hot sauce
Salt and pepper to taste

Grill until done.

Fried Garfish

Gar filets
Beaten egg or mustard
Flour for coating
Bread crumbs for coating
Cooking oil

Dip filets into mustard or egg, then dredge in an equal mixture of bread crumbs and flour. Fry until golden brown.

Zesty Gar

2 pounds gar meat, chopped into small chunks
1 pound of potatoes, cooked and mashed
2 large onions, chopped fine
1 cup combination of parsley, green onions and celery tops, chopped fine
½ cup mustard, plus additional for coating
½ cup vinegar, plus additional for marinade
Water
Flour
Cooking oil

Marinate the meat for 4 hours in a mixture of half vinegar/half water—enough to cover the meat. Then make a sauce by mixing ½ cup of mustard and ½ cup vinegar. In a food processor, mix fish, potatoes, onions and other vegetables together. Shape the mixture into balls 1½ inches in diameter. Roll in mustard, dredge in flour and fry until golden brown. Serve with sauce.

Garfish Pot Roast

1 cleaned garfish
1 onion, chopped
3 to 4 garlic cloves, chopped
1 bell pepper, chopped
Cooking oil

Salt and pepper to taste
Water
Cooked rice

Mix onion, pepper and garlic in a bowl. Make slits in gar and stuff with
mixture. Season the roast well, then heat oil in skillet and brown gar on
all sides. Add a cup of water (part wine or beer, perhaps) and cook
uncovered over medium heat for an hour while adding water to make
gravy. Serve over rice.

Gar Roast

Garfish roast
¼ cup onion and garlic (or shallots), finely minced
Salt
Cayenne pepper
Black pepper
Low-acid vinegar
Cooked rice

Take a garfish roast and slit it vertically every inch or so. Then mince
onion and garlic and combine with salt, peppers, and a shot of vinegar
and stuff pockets with the spices. Season the whole thing with more salt,
black and cayenne peppers, and bake for 45 minutes to an hour at 350
degrees. Make gravy with the drippings. Serve over rice.

Spicy Creole Garfish

3 to 4 pounds garfish steaks
¼ cup cooking oil
16-ounce can of tomatoes
8-ounce can tomato sauce
½ cup onion, chopped
¼ cup green onion, chopped
½ cup bell pepper, chopped
3 tablespoons hot pepper, chopped
1 teaspoon hot sauce
⅓ cup garlic, minced

2 stalks celery, chopped
2 tablespoons fresh parsley, chopped
⅓ cup water
Cooked rice (optional)

Heat oil until it pops when you flick some water in it, then put garfish in, turn temperature down a bit and brown gar on both sides for 1 to 1½ minutes. Take gar out, add onions, peppers, celery, garlic and parsley. Sauté vegetables. Put fish back in, add mixture of tomatoes, tomato sauce, hot sauce and water. Simmer uncovered for 30 minutes. Serve over rice if desired.

Steamed Garfish

2 to 2½ pounds garfish (or two filets)
2 garlic cloves
Zest of one lemon
3 cups dry white wine
12 peppercorns
2 bay leaves
Salt
Pepper
Water

Sauce:

1 small bunch of fresh parsley
2 garlic cloves
2 tablespoons lemon juice
1 egg yolk
Salt
⅛ teaspoon pepper
¼ cup corn oil
6 tablespoons olive oil

Peel and crush garlic and put in a big skillet. Grate lemon zest into skillet and add wine, 5 cups water, parsley stems, peppercorns, bay leaves, and 1 teaspoon of salt. Bring to a boil, then lower heat and simmer for 10 minutes, partially covered. Add garfish and simmer for 15 minutes, partially covered, until fish is tender at its thickest point. Leave fish in mixture and cool to room temperature, approximately 2 hours, or cover and refrigerate in liquid all day.

To make sauce, take a third of a cup of parsley leaves (firmly packed) and mince into the garlic. Whisk lemon juice in a bowl with the egg yolk, parsley leaves, ¼ teaspoon salt, and pepper until smooth. Slowly stir in oils and refrigerate.

When it's time to eat, take fish out of poaching liquid, cut into half-inch slices, drizzle with sauce and serve cold, or at room temperature, immediately.

Garfish Cochon de New Iberia

5 pounds gar filets
Cooking oil
3 pounds ground pork
1 yellow onion, chopped
1 bell pepper, chopped
1 stalk celery, chopped
3 cloves garlic, chopped
2 tablespoons hot sauce
1 teaspoon black pepper
2 tablespoons salt
½ teaspoon oregano
½ teaspoon dill
2 eggs
½ cup bread crumbs
Flour
Cornmeal

Heat oil to 350 degrees and grind filets in food processor until they are the consistency of ground beef. Put in bowl and mix pork, vegetables, spices, eggs, and bread crumbs. Make balls and roll in equal mixture of flour and cornmeal. Fry until golden brown.

You can also shape into patties and barbecue on grill for 20 to 25 minutes, basting occasionally with your favorite sauce.

Mixture can also be used for stuffing poultry, cabbage, peppers, etc.

Garfish Tempura

    1 to 2 pounds boneless gar meat
Cornstarch
Egg
Black pepper
1 tablespoon butter
¼ cup sliced mushrooms
¼ cup chopped green onions
1 tablespoon grated fresh ginger
2 tablespoons soy sauce
2 or 3 tablespoons cooking oil

Heat oil in pan and whisk an egg white in a bowl with a pinch of pepper until it gets frothy. Coat gar meat in cornstarch, dip in egg white and fry on both sides until golden brown.

    To make the sauce, sauté mushrooms and green onions in butter, then stir in ginger and soy sauce. Drizzle over sizzling gar.

Garfish Spitzviche

    2 fresh gar filets (not frozen)
At least 6 limes, maybe more
½ cup chopped red onion
1 chopped hot pepper
2 or 3 tomatoes
Sea salt
Cayenne spice
2 tablespoons fresh mint leaves, chopped
Fresh cilantro
1 fresh avocado
Fresh dill

Refrigerate gar filets, and when they're good and cold, cut into finger-sized strips. In a glass casserole dish, combine fresh-squeezed lime juice, onions, pepper, one chopped tomato, mint, a couple of teaspoons of salt, and dash of cayenne. Mix with a wooden spoon (don't use any metal). Drop in gar strips, cover dish with plastic wrap, and marinate in refrigerator for an hour or two.

Take gar out of mixture, drain off marinade and throw it away. Chop up a tomato, avocado, and cilantro to make salsa, and plop on top of fish. Garnish with dill.

Thai Fishcakes with Cucumber Relish

1 pound gar meat, de-boned
2 tablespoons red curry paste
2 tablespoons fish sauce
1 tablespoon flour
1 egg, beaten
½ cup thinly sliced green beans
¼ cup chopped onion
½ cup bread crumbs
Vegetable oil
½ cup equal mix of cornmeal and flour
1 cup vinegar (white or wine)
1 cup sugar
splash of fish sauce
1 large cucumber
4 red chilies (or use a combination of other hot peppers)
½ cup roasted peanuts, chopped
½ cup basil or cilantro, minced
Garlic chili sauce (commercially prepared)

Chop up fish, then put in food processor and mix it into a paste. Add curry, fish sauce, flour, and egg, and process. Transfer to a bowl and stir in beans, onions and bread crumbs. With wet hands, form patties that are 2½ inches in diameter and ¾-inch thick. Dredge in cornmeal/flour mixture and fry in hot oil until brown on both sides.

To make the cucumber relish, combine vinegar, sugar and fish sauce in a saucepan over medium heat. Bring to a boil and cook for 1 minute, stirring frequently. Remove from heat and bring to room temperature. Meanwhile peel the cucumber, scrape out seeds, and cut into small cubes. Add cucumber, peppers, peanuts and basil or cilantro to the liquid mixture. Serve over fish with garlic chili sauce.

Author and his six-foot-five, 106-pound gator gar, Trinity River, Texas. Photo by Eric Tumminia.

Mark Spitzer is assistant professor of writing at the University of Central Arkansas, managing editor of the *Exquisite Corpse Annual,* and a lifelong, passionate fisherman.

He's the author of a number of novels, story collections, and poetry collections, including *Age of the Demon Tools, Riding the Unit: Selected Nonfiction, 1994–2004, Chum,* and *Bottom Feeder.* He has also published a number of translations, including works by Georges Bataille, Blaise Cendrars, and Louis-Ferdinand Céline. He was a past resident of Paris's famous Shakespeare and Company bookstore, where he honed his translation skills. An essay in the *Yale Anglers' Journal* won a First Place Prose Prize. He was a recent guest on a television episode of Animal Planet's *River Monsters.* He lives in Conway, Arkansas, with his wife, Robin Becker, and two pet gars.